Stepping Stones to a Happy Life
Finding Positivity and Power in Everyday Life

Nadia Jaffery

Nadia Jaffery

CHAPTER LISTING

Stepping Stones to a Happy Life

Introduction

Hello and thank you for choosing this book to further your understanding of your own emotions.

Life can be a difficult journey that we must all learn to navigate. Unfortunately, when we are born, we aren't handed a manual with all the instructions we will ever need. This means that we grow up to be adults and sometimes we find ourselves needing some guidance to navigate the rough waters that lay in front of us. This is where this guide comes in!

I understand the many difficulties that come to us through a lifetime of experiences and I want to make it easier for you to navigate the rough waters of life. I want you to learn how to find true happiness and overcome challenges and adversities that you might face. Nothing in life is black and white, instead, life comes to us in a spectrum of colors and we must learn to embrace every single one.

One of the most grounding things you can do is to remind yourself that everyone in this world has been through heartache, pain, and disappointment. Our feelings aren't singular to us alone and in fact, there are many others who have felt the same aches that we have. This guide uses quotes from some of the greats who have been in your shoes before and offers some wise advice about how to see yourself through times where you struggle. I don't guarantee that you will never struggle in life again, but that you will have better coping methods for the situations that life throws at you.

If you are tired of living a *laissez-faire* life and letting it pass you by while you feel you have no control, then give this guide a read. You will find some great techniques to ground you and some sound advice regarding your emotions.

Chapter one focuses on the idea of happiness; a strange concept in this world that we often think there is some great secret behind. I am going to revolutionize the way that you view happiness and hopefully make it easier for you to achieve.

Chapters two, three, and four are all focused on overcoming the difficulties that life presents to us. These can come in the form of a challenge, loss, or even fear. I want you to find ways to overcome the barriers that might hold you back in life. I want you to explore the good that exists in this world and how you can take advantage of every opportunity presented to you without being overcome by fear or dread.

Finally, in chapter six, I will go more in-depth about the importance of finding peace in your life. Peace can wash over your body and completely transform the way that you think about the world. I want to impart to you the wisdom of great people and their tactics for finding peace in this busy world.

These quotes are going to lead you down the path to a fulfilling life. But you need to do more than simply read the quote and explanation. You have to incorporate the quote into your life. To help you utilize this book to its full potential, I have created a guide:

Get inspired every day. This book is filled with inspirational quotes that can make you feel inspired every day. Take time out of your morning to read at least one passage from this book. You can read any quote you want. For example, if you wake up one morning and want to feel more at peace, then you should review one of the quotes about peace. If you are suffering through the loss of a loved one, you will turn to a quote about loss.

Don't stop your morning ritual until you read each quote. If you read one quote a day and start incorporating it into your life, you will spend 50 mornings reading a part of this book. By then, you have created a whole new world for yourself, family, friends, co-workers, and everyone else who is a part of your day. You also created a habit, one that you should continue by reading more inspirational quotes within your life. You can also choose to re-read this book. It's always a good idea to keep these inspirational quotes fresh in your mind.

Find a way to relate to each passage of this book. Each passage holds a quote, explanation, and a way you can incorporate it into your life. Use this information to relate the passage to your life. Once you accomplish this, you will remember the quote and use it to change your situation and life. This is one of the best ways to get the most out of this book.

You need to be consistent. Don't allow one morning to go by that you don't read a quote. Place two to three minutes into your morning routine to pick up this book, find a quote, and read. The passages in this book shouldn't take you longer than a minute to read, allowing you time to process the information and relate it to your life. Take a little time to reflect after reading the passage as this will help you incorporate the information into your life.

Don't let fear stop you in your tracks. You might find that some of the quotes are challenging. This is good as it will send you soaring onto your path of fulfillment. It will help you reach your best self and believe that you can accomplish anything you set your mind to. Don't allow fear to take control of you when it comes to bringing these quotes into your life.

This book is not just your regular quote book. It is a book that is going to dive into the quotes by giving you explanations. It is going to allow you to tie these quotes into your emotions, so you can relate and learn how to reach your fulfilling life. It is a book that will not only teach you how to reach it, but also how to maintain this type of lifestyle. Some of the topics discussed in this book are not going to be easy. But they are topics that you need to understand and learn about so you can grow and reach your best self or your fulfilling life.

I hope that you find joy and entertainment through this guide. I hope that this guide helps you find your best self, so you can feel that you are leading a fulfilling life. This is a goal that everyone wants to reach, whether they discuss it or not. Life is full of challenges and the world is full of negativity. This makes it hard for you to overcome these factors and lead a life that makes you feel like you have reached your purpose and you are leading a fulfilling life. I hope this guide provides you with a stable basis for grounding your emotions. Happy reading!

Chapter 1: Happiness

Quote #1

"I discovered that joy is not the negation of pain, but rather acknowledging the presence of pain and feeling happiness in spite of it."

- *Lupita Nyong'O.*

Happiness is often thought to be dependent on good things happening to us. Have you ever found yourself feeling sad, dismissive or even upset because of all the misfortune you remember happening in your life? We tend to become hyper-focused on the idea that our lives should always be meaningful and filled with happy moments.

Our emotions can be complicated, and a cesspool of different thoughts and feelings contributes to how we feel at any given moment. A key factor that so many people forget is that the way we feel is not how everyone else around us will feel. One event can bring on two completely different emotions in people. Here is the simple truth about happiness: sadness and pain in our lives do not negate our happy moments. It takes time to wrap our heads around this concept: that simply because you have been sad in your life does not mean you cannot be happy.

Life brings with it many different types of heartaches and pains. We might experience the loss of a loved one, the loss of a home, and even the loss of a sentimental item. We might experience physical or mental pain that creates tension and unhappiness in our lives. There is bound to be at least one thing that makes the memory of our time here on Earth unpleasant.

The average human has more than one experience that they can use to wallow in self-pity.

There comes a time in your life where you need to acknowledge that you are hurting. You need to realize that there might be some pain that you will always carry with you, and then you need to embrace being happy despite that pain. Expecting life to always go your way and always fill you with happy emotions is unrealistic and a recipe for some unhappy emotions. You show true power and control over your life when you can acknowledge that yes, something has hurt you and despite that you choose happiness.

Choosing happiness can be difficult at first. We are conditioned to let our emotions have some rules over what we do and when we do it, however, the truth is that we do have control over our response to situations.

You are not subservient to the emotions you are feeling, and you can find happiness in spite of the pain that an event is bringing up inside you. Simply look in the mirror and understand that you cannot live in sadness because a moment of your life did not induce happiness. Choose every single day that you will let happiness control your smiles and your actions towards others, not the bitterness that life brings with it. You will be able to feel true happiness when you allow yourself to believe that the sad moments of life make the happy moments shine that much brighter.

We often ruin many days for ourselves by letting negative emotions rule at the forefront of our minds because this is how we have been taught to live. You can change. You can exact that change in a generation of people. You can do all of this simply by choosing to be happy in the face of pain and showing others that they too can be happy in the face of pain. You might not be happy every single day of your life, but you can certainly make sure that you are happy most of those days.

Quote #2

"Happiness is not something you postpone for the future; it is something you design for the present."

- *Jim Rohn.*

Have you ever found yourself thinking that tomorrow will be better? That there will be a reason to smile in the future and that today you simply need to wallow? Thoughts like this can lead to a very serious pattern of unhappiness because instead of embracing joy we are promising it to tomorrow.

Stop holding out for the happiness that tomorrow might bring and start designing your happiness in today's life. We are never promised a second chance or a second tomorrow and there is no way to guarantee that we will see the sunrise over the horizon tomorrow. Imagine if you departed this world, and the last emotion you grasped onto was a negative one because you were hoping to be happier tomorrow?

Stop holding out hope for tomorrow and pinning your feelings on a day that has yet to arrive. Focus on the present and start designing and creating your happiness now. Set a plan in action if you struggle to find your happiness then begin to create it for yourself in other ways. You cannot keep hoping for tomorrow to make you happy. Especially if you enact no changes in your own movements to bring that happiness to you. Emotions are not sedentary, and you also need to move towards the emotions that you want to feel. Yes, the pain will always be a part of this life, but you can choose to react differently to this pain. For example, if you know that watching a program on television brings a smile to your face then make a plan. Set a date with yourself so that you can look forward to tomorrow with anticipation and happiness. If you like receiving kind words, leave yourself a sticky note to wake up to. If you start doing small things to plan for your own happiness then inevitably, you will find happiness now and not tomorrow or the next day.

Putting off your happiness for another day is allowing yourself to wallow in negative emotions. You are not being the cause of change that your life needs. What would you say to a friend who told you that they would try to be happy in the future? You need to take a more active role in your own happiness and create it rather than wait for it. Don't sit idly by while life passes you by, instead make plans for today. Set those plans into action today. Give yourself every reason to find happiness today. Stop using tomorrow as an excuse because today is the only real present you are given. Use that to your advantage and participate in actions that perpetuate your own happiness.

It is possible to be happy today. You know that it is possible, you just need to allow yourself to see this possibility and then make determined steps towards it. I get it. It is easy to passively allow life to flow around you. Living this way, however, won't see you the happiness that you are aiming for. A life of inactivity breeds the same emotions. You need to start changing your own patterns in order to find the happiness that you are looking for. Change patterns within you and make plans. Start out with a small plan and then steadily grow your plan. Perhaps today you are writing a sticky note that will make you smile in the morning and three months from now you are planning that trip you always meant to take but never quite found the right time for. Don't let life pass you by while you hope it hands you happiness on a silver platter. This won't happen. Seek your happiness, plan for your happiness, and then carry out those plans.

Quote #3

"Folks are usually about as happy as they make their minds up to be."

- *Abraham Lincoln.*

If you struggle with negative emotions on a daily basis, the time might come to ask yourself who is really at fault for your sadness or unhappiness. Abraham Lincoln said this quote many years ago, and its basis still holds true today. For most people being happy is not about the outside effects of life, but rather how they choose to feel. There will inevitably be days where sad things occur or your heart is heavy, however that should not impact your life until the end of your time.

Have you ever felt that no matter what you did or said, no matter what anyone else said or did, and no matter what you changed, you were unhappy? Now, have you ever given thought to the idea that maybe you enjoy being upset or sad? I know. You are probably thinking, "Who in their right mind enjoys being sad?" However, there comes a time when you are unable to find happiness in your life that you begin to question if you truly are at the crux of your own problem. Often times you will find that yes, you are your own problem.

We are our own worst enemies when it comes to being happy. We are so set on a certain path that life should follow that any deviation from that plan begins to ferment seeds of unhappiness. It is easy to find ourselves glum when we end up in a completely different place than we imagined in our idealistic youth. Life takes many turns and not all of them are the ones that we planned for ourselves. However, we can do two things about this. We can sit and wallow and allow the bad feelings to ferment, or we can start to enact change and we can choose to be happy.

If you don't want to be happy, then guess what? You will find that **10 times out of 10** you are not happy. Happiness is largely created by your own mindset. So, when you only allow yourself to bask in a negative mindset you won't allow yourself to be happy. Start changing that perception of yourself now. Right in this moment. Don't wait until tomorrow or the next day. You need to decide for yourself that you are going to be happy and then take a hold of that happiness. Abraham Lincoln was not throwing words to the wind when he said you are only as happy as you allow yourself to be. Those are true words and there are millions of people out in this world who can change their interactions with the world if they just grabbed happiness.

Try and keep a notebook or mentally chide yourself when you feel that you are being pessimistic about the world around you. Force your mind to take a more positive take and allow yourself to be happy. You don't have to feel guilty for finding happiness or enjoyment in a moment. Embrace this happiness and then carry it onto the next thing that you do. At the end of the day, only you can choose whether you are going to be happy or not. Outside people have no influence on how you feel and when you feel it. If you allow yourself the chance to be truly happy you might surprise yourself by finding real happiness in almost every little thing that you do.

Quote #4

"Joy is what happens to us when we allow ourselves to recognize how good things really are."

- *Marianne Williamson.*

Sometimes bad seasons come into our lives and they put us in a funk. It can be hard to recognize when these bad seasons are finally over and the sun has come back out in its brilliance. I know that you want to feel joy in your life, maybe you have even said those exact words out loud before. What does joy look like? It can be easy to tell someone to start being happy or to go after their happiness, but how do we allow ourselves to finally see that the bad times are over and the good are here?

Practical changes are easier to enact than the less tangible idea of "just be happy!" One of the most important things to leave yourself open to are new experiences and new ideas. It doesn't matter where you are in life, you can always learn something new or try something new. This creates massive change in your life when you open yourself up to a new mindset.

Difficult times in our lives are often carried on for far longer than they should be, and this is most often because we allow ourselves to live in the same rut that we do when we are in our darkest times. Changing our routine, or even realizing that our routine has begun to change on its own can bring in the first rays of happiness. You want to keep creating new experiences so that you give yourself a chance to live.

Sometimes you need to take a moment and

collect your thoughts about where you are in life. Are you still sad? Do you really think that there is nothing good in your life? Take an afternoon out and after some careful reflection physically write out a list of the things that you are thankful for. This includes anything that brings you joy and happiness. This life is never as bad as we make it out to be and there is often a plethora of things that bring us joy. We simply ignore them because they don't fit the criteria for our dark days. Misery loves company and often this company is your own thoughts and feelings. You drag yourself down when you only allow yourself to bask in the negative.

I challenge you to take one moment and take stock of where you are in life. Are you positive that there is nothing to smile about in your life? If you give yourself half the chance then I am confident that you will find a host of things, people, and memories that bring you joy. Life is not as bad as we sometimes make it out to be. We have pretended for years that being upset or sad is par for the course. However, it really isn't. You can look around and realize that life is filled with moments of happiness and joy, you simply need to allow yourself to live in those moments.

Even if you have hit a bad season in your life, that doesn't make it a bad life. Finding joy despite the moments of disparity is important, you need to learn to replenish your soul with joy or you will become jaded with the world. Once you have a list of reasons to find that you are in a good place in life repeat this list to yourself daily. Let every good thought and memory roll around in your mind. You might find that you tackle the day with much more optimism than you previously thought was possible.

Quote #5

"We can't control the world. We can only (barely) control our own reactions to it. Happiness is largely a choice, not a right or entitlement."

- *David C. Hill.*

You have probably learned by now that the world doesn't owe you anything. In fact, the more we wish it did, the harder life seems to kick us in the behind. You cannot control what happens around you, but you can control how you react to it. We like to blame our emotions for our actions — particularly in the heat of the moment. The truth is that we have total and complete control over each of our actions even when they are fueled by emotions.

You cannot go through life using emotions as an excuse to act and do as you please. Similarly, you cannot blame your emotions for you feeling sad about where you are in life. You have a choice over exactly how these emotions affect you and how you can move forward with the emotion present in your mind. I get it. Sometimes this can be hard to put into practice. It is tempting to allow ourselves to wallow in what our emotions tell us is an appropriate action. However, when that fog clears and you are all that is left standing, you have to take eventual responsibility for the way that you acted or the things that you said and did. Nobody is entitled to feel happy. It is not given to you as a birthright and you don't earn the right to be happy through living your life. The other caveat is that nobody is responsible for ensuring your happiness. Nobody but you, that is. You are the only person who is both responsible and in control of your own happiness. If this sounds like tough love right now, then yes, it is. It is time to stop letting your head drift away in the clouds and to start putting in hard thought about how you let your emotions control you.

For example, when you get angry at a situation you have control over what you say and do. Being angry is not an excuse to say or do hurtful things. There are times when your anger might have pushed you to want to say the most extreme thing, however, you need to exercise your control over this emotion. Don't misinterpret me here, I think that you should acknowledge your emotions, however, you don't have to act with your emotions. Acknowledge that something made you angry, say that it upset you but act in a way that benefits you and others that are involved in the situation.

The reason I say happiness is a choice is simply that it is. You can fester in your anger, or you could acknowledge it for what it is and then choose to be happy. Choose to learn, let the anger go, and allow your happiness to take over. The world is a big place and a lot of unsavory things happen in it from day to day, but this doesn't mean that we should expect life to produce our happiness for us. On the contrary, we should be the pioneers at the forefront of building our own happiness every single day. Build your own happiness and stop expecting it from the world around you, I promise you will find you smile a lot more when you do so.

When the world hands you lemons, **stop fighting it**. Allow the lemons to come in and if making lemonade makes you happy then do just that. Don't let your light be snuffed out because of a momentary blight in your day. There are so many things out of your control in this world, at least you can control the way that you respond to the world around you.

Quote #6

"When one door of happiness closes, another opens; but often we look so long at the closed door that we do not see the one which has been opened for us."

- *Helen Keller.*

I am sure that in your lifetime you have heard the phrase "when one door closes another opens." While you might want to roll your eyes, there is a truth that lies in these words. Often there are misfortunes — or at least perceived misfortunes — that happens in this life and it can feel like a door we had waited our whole lives to open is suddenly slamming shut in our face. What do we do about this? How do we combat this?

For most people, the answer is to wail and bemoan the closed door. They spend so long staring at the missed opportunity that they waste any other opportunities that might rise around them. Don't be the person who bangs against the closed door begging it to open. Be the person who takes stock of what happened and then actively starts searching out their next opportunity.

Life will bring with it sadness, joys, losses, and triumphs. It is inevitable and honestly a fact that we should truly embrace. How do you recognize true happiness if you have never experienced a rain cloud? How do you know that your smile is genuine if you have never cried a tear? You need to understand that not everything you want to work out is going to work out. Yes, sometimes there is a reason for this, and other times there are no reasons. Life simply happens. You have two choices. One — which is the choice most people make — is to bemoan the closed door of happiness. Two — which you would be far better off making — is to open up your eyes and heart for the next door or even window of happiness.

Life is ultimately what you make of it. If you cry over the closed door you might look up too late to see that other door that had opened for you close too. Don't live your life blind to the opportunities that are presented to you. Rather accept the things that have been denied to you and reach out for the opportunities that are within your reach. There is always another door or another window. You always have another road to take. It is up to you to make use of these avenues and secure your happiness.

Don't worry if you don't manage to find the happiness right away. It takes time to take you out of thought processes that you have been conditioned to believe in. Our society makes us believe that we should lament the closed door, but you should find happiness in the potential door instead. Practice focusing on the positive things in your life whenever something does not work out for you. Keep these fresh in your mind or even write them down if that helps you out. Don't become a victim of misfortune, rather pave your own path to the new door that is waiting for you to step through. When you take this approach you will find that your doors are not simply limited to one, but that you have opportunity growing from multiple sites all at once, you only need to foster this growth. Life is not about one path to happiness, there are several paths to happiness. Keep this in mind as you traverse the many journeys life offers you.

Quote #7

"Cry. Forgive. Learn. Move on. Let your tears water the seeds of your future happiness."
- *Steve Maraboli.*

Has someone hurt you in the past? Have you found yourself sink into a depression and struggle to move on from the way that they slighted you? So often we find ourselves the victims of actions that have been perpetrated against us. Maybe your spouse left you, you found out about an extra-marital affair, you lost a loved one or any other various scenes that cause hurt to happen deep in the heart. It doesn't matter what it was, what matters is that it happened, and it hurt you.

It can be tempting to sit in our hurt and let it consume us. To allow the pain of another's actions — maybe even our own actions — to override every other emotion that we feel. In fact, we can become stagnant, only sitting in one place when we allow ourselves to be dragged down by negative thoughts. The only person that this is negatively affecting is you, yourself. You are stealing from your own joy when you allow your mind to focus on the negative emotions. Earlier in this chapter, I spoke to you about the way that you have ultimate control over your response to a situation. That is still very much true and something that you want to think about with the words of Steve Maraboli.

I will **always** encourage you to acknowledge your emotions and allow them to be a part of you. In fact, you should let yourself feel every emotion inside you. If someone has hurt, you allow yourself to feel that hurt. If you are sad, allow yourself the tears that you need. Never bottle up feelings inside of you. However, once you have embraced your emotions then it is time for you to start moving forward. Keep putting one foot in front of the other until you have a clear picture of where you want to go. Every situation that you are exposed to will teach you something. You will learn something new, you will grow, and you will have a different perspective on that matter in life than you did before.

Allow yourself to cry, allow yourself to forgive. You need to move on from the pain in life so that you can find happiness. True growth comes when you use your exposure to pain to propel you to a more prosperous future. You can't expect a life without some dull corners, but you can expect to make a better life for yourself from the knowledge that you have learned.

I know, this seems easier said than done. That is par for the course with most things in life. It takes practice, dedication, and commitment in order to effect any real change in your life. I know you want to live in a more positive light. You wouldn't be reading this if you didn't. The path toward this positive light is bumpy at the best of times. However, I am confident that you can take control of your future by allowing the experiences of today to educate you. There is happiness to be found even on the darkest of days.

So, cry as much as you need to cry, and forgive every person who you have ever felt has done you wrong. Not for them. Not for you. But for your future happiness. There is nothing to be gained from holding onto bitterness, and everything to be gained from inviting happiness. You will never be truly happy until you see the past as a lesson, not a mistake.

Quote #8

"If you aren't grateful for what you already have, what makes you think that you would be happy with more?"
- *Roy T. Bennett.*

As defined in the dictionary, gratefulness is a feeling of appreciation for something that we have received or that has been done toward us. Often unhappiness is bred from a discontentment in our lives. Whether this is with where we are in life or what we have in life, we are left unhappy. It becomes easy to find faults with what we have or what we are doing, and we forget to look at what we do have.

For example, while it might sound mundane, truly having the smallest things life has to offer is something we should be grateful for. I'm by no means suggesting that you settle for less than you want or less than you believe you deserve. What I am saying is that you should find happiness in what you already have. Gaining more objects, possessions, notoriety is not going to satisfy you or soothe your soul if you can't find peace in what you already have.

Happiness is about more than just feeling joy. You want to be able to feel content and happy for where you are in your life — genuinely content. This means that you take the time to appreciate the roof that you have over your head, the meals that you get to eat, the car you get to drive, the vacations you get to take or plan. Appreciate any family you have, any partners you make, the work that you do, or even the simple fact that you have a job. For example, you don't have to love the job you are doing in order to be grateful to have it. This is what I mean about being grateful for what you currently have. When you can show appreciation for your current station in life then you are ten times more likely to enjoy it as you raise that station. On the flip side of this, if you continue to be sour about where you are and negative about the things you have accumulated then it is unlikely that more material possessions or a different partner will make you appreciate them.

Stop saying "one day when I get there" and start taking accountability for what you have now. Find the joy in the little things. Write out an entire list of everything that you are grateful for. Sometimes we find ourselves in spots where it is hard to find gratefulness for our current station in life. I understand that, however, you cannot let this carry on indefinitely. You need to take stock of what is around you and practice showing gratefulness. It might be hard at first, but take it one day, one thing at a time. For example, it can be as simple as the fact that you are grateful that you are still living. Appreciate your life, every cell that makes up who you are and then move on to be grateful for something else that is important to you. If you take it one step at a time you will make great changes in a short period of time.

There is never a weakness in gratefulness, and you are not settling for less when you show appreciation for what you have. You will open yourself up to bigger and better avenues while finding happiness in what you currently have.

Quote #9

"Time you enjoy wasting is not wasted time."
- *Marthe Troly-Curtin.*

Have you ever felt like every minute of every day you HAVE to be doing something? Even in your free time you have to find some way to occupy it, some grand thing to do or you are just wasting your life. We have been taught that the absence of productivity is an evil thing. That we should never be idle, never relax. We have come to fear wasted time as a generation because we think that we are allowing life to pass us by if we do not occupy our every minute.

I want you to take a step back from the way you have always been taught to feel about time. I want you to take a moment to enjoy your life, enjoy your time. Whether you enjoy time by watching television, laying on the couch, reading a book, or simply doing absolutely nothing! I want you to take your personal time and really start enjoying it. Here's the secret about life that not many people want you to know as long as you are enjoying your life then you are not wasting any time at all.

Unhappiness can stem from the pressures that we put on ourselves to fill up our time. However, at the end of the day what makes you happy is all that counts. You need to let the pressures to fill your time fade away and take enjoyment in the simple things you do, even if those simple things mean you lay on the couch all afternoon.

You cannot call it waste as long as you find some happiness in it. Do you want to know when you waste your time? When you fill it up with things that have no meaning to you. If you are only allowing your life to pass you by and not taking pleasure in it then, by the very definition of it, you are wasting your time! To partake in any activity that you derive no pleasure from means that you are wasting time. I am not talking about the jobs and chores we have to do, but more so the choices we make with our free time. For example, let us say that you went to a party you have no interest in going to. You didn't enjoy your time there and you were generally miserable. That is a huge amount of time you wasted when you could have found happiness doing something you loved — even if that something was laying on the couch. Doing anything that brings you joy fulfills your time and is a good use of the minutes we are given on this earth. Don't let anyone make you feel bad for not following their path to enjoyment. Revel in what you like doing and do it!

There is no recipe for happiness. No certain rules and restrictions to follow. You make your own happiness. You need to forge your own path, not by what you think the world says you should be doing. So, take one afternoon a week and waste your time doing whatever brings you the most joy! At the end of the day as long as you feel joy then your time is never wasted. How can you waste time when you love what you are doing?

Quote #10

"Thousands of candles can be lit from a single candle, and the life of the candle will not be shortened. Happiness never decreases by being shared."

- *Buddha (Gautama Buddha, n.d.)*

It is easy to want to be selfish when we find happiness. Once you truly feel happy you want to cling on to this feeling for as long as possible. There is nothing wrong with that. Everyone deserves to feel the happiness they are craving. What happens when we aim to take that happiness away from someone else?

You should not light your candle off of the misery that someone else feels. Sometimes we act without thinking (remember I said earlier how we are always in control of our actions? This is true and takes practice) and we can cut someone down with both our words and actions. Making someone else feel small won't make ourselves feel better, especially not in the long run. You want to be happy, and so does that other person. Your thoughts and feelings are not the only ones out in the world. However, I want to let you in on a secret. Often, we find joy through making others smile. Our happiness can be derived from the happiness of others.

So, instead of snuffing out someone else's candle try and be a positive force in their day. Share your happiness in the hopes that it travels to them. You will feel better overall when you have helped someone else find their light with your own light.

Sometimes people are apprehensive to share their happiness because they feel like someone might take it away from them. However, you are in control of your actions and feelings. As long as you CHOOSE to be happy, no one can take away your happiness from you. This gives you the freedom that you need to continue spreading happiness. You can do this in many ways from more simple acts of kindness to those around you to volunteer with those who are less fortunate in this world, to creating and effecting change in the world around you. Try and do one random kind act today, like telling a coworker or a friend that they look nice. Every day add to this act of kindness and compound on it. Your happiness will be returned to you tenfold.

- -

Chapter 2: Overcoming Challenges

Quote #1

"As with the butterfly, adversity is necessary to build character in people."

- *Joseph B. Wirthlin.*

Butterflies aren't born with their beautiful wings. When they first emerge into this world, they are fat, wriggly little caterpillars. It takes weeks for them to grow and metamorphose into a beautiful butterfly. They go through a lot of changes before they show their true colors. The same is true with humans. Before our true selves are revealed, we go through many challenges that shape us. Every day, every month, and every year we go through adversities that change our perceptions of both ourselves and the world.

Challenges are a natural part of this life. You will inevitably encounter some form of challenges as you grow and mature. You might find that some of these challenges are easier than others, while some make it hard for you to want to face the day. You have to understand that there is nothing wrong with being challenged in life. It is normal and everyone goes through their own set of personal challenges. You can do two things about your own challenges. You can learn how to overcome and grow from them, or you can run from them.

However, I want you to keep in mind that you didn't get to where you are today without challenges. You have experienced both small and large challenges in order to become the brilliant human being that you currently are. Unlike butterflies, who go through one metamorphosis, human beings are constantly changing and evolving. Every new experience that you go through will shape you in a different way. For example, a past relationship might teach you what to avoid in a future relationship.

You need to feel comfortable with the idea of overcoming a challenge. This doesn't come easily. If there is something you are struggling with right now, write it down in a notebook, journal, or even simply on a sticky note. Keep a list of the challenges that you perceive are ahead of you and then draw up a plan of action. Make sure that each challenge is listed either in order of importance to you or in order of difficulty. You have free reign with this so create the list as it suits you. Then, take the top challenge and put your plan of action behind it. Carry it out. Note the changes that you experience as you overcome the challenge or difficulty. It can be small. For example, if you are struggling with depression, then getting out of bed might be a difficult thing to do every day. That is a daily challenge that you are overcoming. Figure out a plan of action to prompt you to get out of bed. Then try and enact it. Applaud yourself if you make it. Even if you only made it out of bed for five minutes or if it took you one hour to work up the strength to pull yourself out. As the butterfly shows off its brilliant colors, take pride in your own accomplishments because they do matter, and they make you who you are.

Your challenges won't look the same as everyone else's. We all battle with our own uncertainties and flaws. Your adversities do truly become you; they make you and they shape you. You should always embrace this. You never know exactly how your problems are going to shape you, but you can control how you respond to them. Continue to climb mountains and you will continue to grow as a person. Remember, like the butterfly, your most beautiful phase has not come yet.

Quote #2

"Challenges are what make life interesting; overcoming them is what makes life meaningful." - *Joshua J. Marine (Joshua J. Marine Quotes, n.d.)*

Have you ever thought to yourself, "wow! my life is boring." Or do you ask life to merely give you a break from the drama that it seems to enjoy imploding into your world? How do you handle this? How do you find a balance between an interesting life and a meaningful life?

Your life will always be interesting to some degree because there will always be something for you to overcome or to look forward to. If you find that you cannot think of a single challenge or obstacle in your life right now (which can be as simple as wanting to change your job) then more than likely you are running away from a challenge you don't feel ready to face. That's okay. However, you do need to understand that sooner or later that challenge will crop up and you will need to find some way to handle it.

In the words of Joshua Marine, the truly meaningful aspects of life come from overcoming the obstacles that we struggle with. This means that you need your challenges, but more than that, you need to overcome your challenges. In the previous quote, we explored the idea that obstacles in life make you who you are and help grow you as a person. Now, we tackle the idea that the challenges you go through as you journey through this life will mean the difference between having a meaningful or interesting life. As I have already said, we all have our own adversities. Unfortunately, we don't always overcome those adversities. This could happen for many reasons. Maybe you're scared or you're unsure of how to move forward with the issue. When we allow ourselves to become stuck in this way the only people that we hurt are ourselves. We stunt both our emotional and mental growth when we refuse to tackle the challenges that lay ahead.

I know that you don't want this to be you. I know that your purpose in life is to flourish and to find meaning within it, I want that for you too. That is why you are going to steadily work to overcome any issue that you face, and you are going to turn your life from merely interesting to meaningful.

It is important to create a meaningful life for yourself for many reasons. However, one of the top reasons I like to remind people of is that your most inspiring actions can stem from the adversity you want to avoid. You might find that the path to inspiring others comes from a tough challenge you conquered. As your challenges change you, you will begin to think critically about the ways that you can apply your learned knowledge to the world. Not everyone has to go through your challenges to have learned from them, they can learn from understanding your journey.

However, not all of our challenges will lead us to inspire those around us. Some of our challenges will fundamentally change the way we see our world, and others will shift how you view a particular issue. No matter what the adversity you face, when you find a way to climb the mountain, you will find a way to add meaning into your existence. I know that this can seem like a very complicated matter but keep reminding yourself that for every challenge there is meaning waiting at the end.

Quote #3

"If you ever find yourself doubting you can make it through a challenge, simply think back to everything you've overcome in the past."

- Karen Salmonsohn (20 Self Love Quotes to Inspire More Positivity and Strong Self Esteem, n.d.).

You might often forget that where you are now is a unique position. I say unique position because you didn't get there by never facing a challenge in your life. You got there through the different things that life has thrown at you. Today, you are a living, breathing human being and you have absolutely experienced a lot throughout your life. That is a simple fact. However, we tend to forget what we have overcome in the past or the challenges that we have conquered when we are faced with new challenges ahead. This is a pivotal mistake we are all guilty of, so don't beat yourself up too badly when you realize you focus too much on what you haven't done and not enough on where you have already succeeded.

If you are struggling with your own capabilities and whether you think you can handle another problem or issue in your life, take a time-out. Yes, time-outs are a valuable asset to keep in mind. Remember that you don't need to let the challenge you are going through consume your life. Step away from it until you are in a better frame of mind to tackle it. I implore you to make sure that you do the work to go back to whatever the adversity was that you were tackling.

Take a moment and write out a list of every challenge you have ever overcome. Include the big ones and the small ones. Every single one of these challenges is something that you have overcome, and you should be proud of yourself for that. Use this time as a period of self-reflection when doubt settles in. You have come through a lot and somehow you have endured. This means that there is a way forward with the next adversity facing you. All you have to do is find it.

Getting discouraged is a serious issue and it can impact your ability to clearly see through the problem. This is why I recommend reminding yourself and looking back at everything you have already been through. So far, you have existed and survived through your worst problems in life. Who is to say that you won't keep doing so? There will always be an issue for you to battle, but you must remind yourself that you haven't lost yet, so why throw in the towel before you've given yourself a real chance to win?

Once you have your list of accomplishments written down, read through them. Remind yourself of everything you had to go through in order to be the person you are today and to be standing where you are. That was no small miracle. It was not dumb luck or chance. That was all you. You have built your life and you are continuing to build it. Don't give up because you feel like you cannot do it. Think back on everything you have accomplished so far and remind yourself that you can do it. Getting yourself into the right mindset is half the battle, so if you can do that then you are halfway there.

Quote #4

"There are no great people in this world, only great challenges which ordinary people rise to meet."

- *William Frederick Halsey, JR. (Acosta, 2014).*

Have you ever thought of someone to look up to and said, "Wow! They're an amazing person." I know I have. In fact, most of the world finds idols to look up to and consider wonderful or amazing. That's nothing new. We don't want to admit however that it is not the person who is amazing but the way they have overcome their greatest challenges that makes them amazing.

Think about why your idol is someone you find amazing. What have they done to inspire you or draw your attention? What kinds of obstacles and challenges have they overcome to be sitting where they are today?

You see, this same kind of logic applies to your own life. You might think that you aren't great or that you will never accomplish the same things that other amazing people have. However, this is simply incorrect. The truth is that everyone in this world is quite ordinary. The challenges that we go through in life and how we rise or fall to meet them is what brings out the extraordinary in us.

Not every challenge brought to you in life is going to be a mountain you will need to climb, but you will find that in the seasons of life there might be one or two challenges that prompt you to rise above yourself. You can do extraordinary things, the same way that the people you look up to have done.

Is there something holding you back? Are there challenges you wish you could simply run away from? I understand how daunting it can be to tell yourself to rise up when you feel like shrinking back. This feeling stems from the idea that you are not "good enough" or "amazing enough" to complete the task ahead of you. This is why you need to shift your thinking. Stop believing that it is the person who is amazing, because it is not. The amazing part is what the person chooses to overcome and how they overcome adversity.

You have the potential to do amazing things too, you simply need to start thinking about yourself in that context. There will be great challenges that present themselves to you throughout your entire life and you need to be ready when they come because you have two options. One, you can run away. Or two, you can rise to the challenge and find ways to become extraordinary by climbing the mountain before you.

Sounds easy, *right?* Of course not. The greatest challenges are never easy. Don't beat yourself up if you feel like you can't do it. However, understand the difference between a momentary lapse of faith in your abilities and running away. You can do this. You know that you can. After all, it is your life, a challenge you are facing and there is no right way to conquer it. Any way that you choose to tackle the challenge will be the right way because it is no one else's challenge but yours. Celebrities and other well-known people are not the only human beings with the capability to do and conquer great things. You are too. Keep reminding yourself daily that you have the potential to do great things as well. You have the potential to be amazing because it is not the man who is born amazing but the adversity, he goes through that molds him into something amazing.

Quote #5

"Being challenged in life is inevitable, being defeated is optional."

- *Roger Crawford.*

Some days the will to carry on is gone from us. We ache to throw in the towel, move away from the "hard stuff" and simply give up. What would life look like if we gave up every time, we felt slightly uncomfortable?

You can't expect to never be challenged in this life. It happens every day. In both small ways and big ways. It is inevitable and you will find yourself being faced with adversity far more than once in your life. Here's the thing about challenges: you always have the choice between success and failure. While things might seem hard, and generally like the situation is out of your hands, those are words we tell ourselves to feel comfortable with giving up.

You have a choice to make with every challenge that you find yourself facing. This is entirely up to you, and contrary to what we often tell ourselves — yes, we do have complete control over the outcome. You don't have to allow your challenges to defeat you or to remain standing while you find a way to circumvent them. This comes down to your mindset.

How are *you* approaching the challenge? How are you devising your plan of action? How are you allowing yourself to feel and speak about the challenge? If you only think negatively towards the challenge, then your head will never be in the right space to overcome it. You will allow yourself to be defeated before you have even had a real chance to tackle the issue. So, the question you might now be thinking is, "How do I combat this?"

Negativity is a state of mind that you can shift; you don't have to live like that. One method I find particularly helpful is to start with meditation. Clear your mind and allow yourself to be calm right before you think about the issue at hand. It helps to let go of the negative emotions and feelings you were holding in. If you're used to meditating, then this should be an easy exercise for you. However, not everyone is used to meditation. You might need to practice meditation a few times before you settle into a routine and truly feel at peace.

Meditation looks different for everyone and you need to find a way that works best for you. Some people like to sit still, others like to walk through a quiet forest or wooded area. The key idea, however, is that you find a quiet and peaceful place to meditate. You need to allow yourself to truly focus on clearing your head. Once you have meditated and found a clear mind, think about how you can positively tackle the challenge ahead of you.

Banish all thoughts of "I can't" and "It won't work." Give yourself positive affirmations about the task at hand. You can do this, you've got this. You are the only person standing in your own way. Sometimes leaving yourself notes to wake up to on your bathroom mirror or even your fridge gives you a chance to start your day with a positive mindset. Trust me when I say that this mindset will be the difference between your success and failure.

Don't let negative thoughts be the reason you feel defeated. You have complete control over the outcome of your challenge. You simply need to put the work in and have a positive mindset so that you can overcome the uphill battle ahead of you. I have faith that when you become more positive about your circumstances you will see an instant change in how you process them and how easily you find yourself mounting those hurdles.

Quote #6

"Strength does not come from what you can do. It comes from overcoming the things you once thought you couldn't."

- Rikki Rogers (Life Quotes, n.d.).

I want to spend a moment here analyzing the words that Rogers uses when describing strength. When we consider strength we think of capable, strong, and formidable. There are a lot of aspects to the word strength and it is important to remember that they don't al refer to physical strength that a person might encounter. For example, your mental and emotional strength are two very important aspects to keep in mind when you are attempting to overcome challenges.

As I have already mentioned to you, your mindset is one of the most important parts of yourself. When you have a negative outlook, you will find it harder to accomplish tasks. When you have a positive mindset all of a sudden there are a host of tasks that become easier for you to perform! It is easy to consider ourselves strong willed or strong natured when we complete those tasks that come easily to us. For example, let us say that you are an adept swimmer with the breaststroke. Placing first in an event that involves the breaststroke is an easy challenge for yourself to overcome because you are positive and confident in your abilities.

However, let us take that same event. The difference is that now you have to compete in the backstroke which is not your strongest swimming style. Suddenly, doubt begins to set in, and you panic as you wonder how you're going to overcome this challenge. The minute you allow yourself to start doubting your abilities is when you start sapping your strength. Now, for a simple moment, imagine that you swam and did well in the backstroke. You succeeded at a challenge you were not sure you could complete. That is where your true strength lies.

No matter what you are doing you, need to be able to handle it with quiet confidence. I am not saying go out there and be arrogant, however I am saying that you should take note of your hard work and your abilities and be positive about them. As Rogers states, there are many things in this life that we are going to doubt if we can do. For example, you might doubt becoming a parent or you might be doubtful about your capabilities in the chosen field of your degree.

Doubt is okay, it happens to the best of us. You don't want to get sucked into the spiral of doubt where you begin to have a negative reflection of yourself. Keep up having a positive attitude and remaining upbeat about where you are going or what you are doing. You will find that as you put one foot in front of the other and keep persevering through all the challenges that life insists on throwing at you that you will find your own true strength.

Attempting to complete a challenge you are familiar with and know the ins and outs is easy. However, growing through adversity and things that you find troubling or difficult and even where you doubt yourself, is where you will show true humility and strength. There are few things in this life that brings more joy to a person than finding the strength to accomplish something they didn't think they could do in the first place.

You're no different. You too will find your strength. The difference is that you need to put in the work to complete the challenge you view as impossible. This means working hard, continuing when you want to give up and brainstorming when a roadblock interferes in your path. Don't give up because you think you CANNOT do it, carry on despite those fears.

Quote #7

"When you meet obstacles with gratitude, your perception starts to shift, resistance loses its power, and grace finds a home within you."

- *Oprah Winfrey (Motivation Mondays: Power of Gratitude, 2019).*

So far, we have talked a lot about the mindset that you approach problems with. It is important to stay positive when you are dealing with a challenge because your mindset will make the difference between the level of difficulty and the ease with which you combat the problem. How do you find gratitude when you are offered problems?

It can be very different to look at the challenges or even merely one challenge that lies ahead and try and be grateful for the uphill battle that is about to take place in your life. No one wants to be faced with the prospect that they are about to encounter difficulties. However, it is crucial that you try your best to view obstacles as opportunities rather than inconveniences. This is the shift in perception that Oprah talks about. Let us say that you are battling against a particularly difficult challenge and every bone in your body is tired of fighting. You adopt the mindset that you have already lost, and you find that with every step you take forward, there is a force that is resisting your progress.

Do you want to know a secret? This resistance that you are encountering is your own negativity. You want to be graceful and grateful to the changes in your life, not resentful. The reason is because your grace will make your problem much easier to tackle. Instead of being obstinate, we invite the problem in and suddenly it becomes opportunity, not something to battle.

There is a lesson to be learned in everything that we go through in life, and no matter how painful those lessons are, we must learn to be grateful that we have learned them as we move onto the next phase in our life. When you are struggling through an issue, try and keep this in mind. Tell yourself that there is a reason you need to learn this lesson for the next challenge ahead, that the information you find out today will be useful down the road in your life. Sometimes it takes years before the reason behind the challenge reveals itself. Other times its application to your life is instantaneous.

Do you want to constantly fight the resistance your challenges give you? Would it not be easier to accept with gratitude the different seasons that life offers you and take away from each season a lesson to carry with you for life? It can be a task all in itself to try and shift your perception to one of gratefulness when life hands you lemons. I find that it is helpful to journal through the different emotions and feelings. Start a journal and write out your feelings about the challenge. Even the negative ones. However, for every negative feeling that you write down I want you to have a positive feeling that you are working toward. For example, if you write down that you are worried you are going to fail at this particular obstacle, combat that by writing down how you anticipate finding the solution to your obstacle.

Use positive emotions to help you be grateful for the obstacle in life. From gratefulness your grace will be borne, and you will handle the obstacle better than you initially expected you would.

Quote #8

"The most difficult thing is the decision to act, the rest is merely tenacity."

- Amelia Earhart (67 Quotes About Overcoming Adversity and Challenges in Your Life, 2019).

Are you going to keep running away from your problems? When do you finally decide that enough is enough and you are going to start facing them head on? The decision to tackle your problems is the first half of the battle that you have. The minute that you have made a plan to act on your challenge then half of your work is done. You would have also completed the hardest part of the battle.

Sometimes we think that putting in the work is where the real challenge comes into play, but we are wrong. When you have an obstacle before you, a flight or fight response is initiated. When you take flight, you don't give yourself an opportunity to best the challenge. However, when you stand your ground and take the option of fight you need to assemble a plan of action and then decide to go through with it. This is far harder than most people think it is. Deciding to do something can be nerve-wracking, and this is where most plans in life tend to stall — the moment between inaction and action.

If you are struggling with adversity in life right now, take a step back and ask yourself, "What am I doing about this?" Don't sit by passively as the challenge engulfs your life, but rather take a more active approach with it. I promise you that once you decide to react to the problem, you will find that putting in the work is a lot easier.

This circles back to your mindset and dedication. Humans are very stubborn creatures by nature. So, once we set our minds to a task more often than not that task is completed. All you have to do is decide what you are going to do about your obstacle. Much easier said than done, I know! Action becomes a lot easier to implement when you already have an idea of what you are going to do and how you are going to do it. If you are struggling with a decision of whether to tackle a problem or let it be, write out a list of pros and cons for yourself. Is it beneficial to you or those around you for you to continue to handle this problem? If it is. then write out your plan of action and decide to go for it! Keep in mind that positivity will help you out tremendously at this point.

The reason you have a flight or fight response is because not every problem or obstacle that comes into your life is one where your action is going to be required. Sometimes, the solution to your obstacle is to let it go and to walk away. This itself can pose a lot of problems for you. However, it comes back down to that decision for action — whether you decide to act by solving the problem or by walking away from the problem. No matter what the decision is, once you make it you will have an easier time doing the required action because that is simply your dedication and tenacity to your actions. The time-consuming part and the difficult part of obstacles is deciding to act. Face this fear head on. It can sometimes help to give yourself a deadline by which to plan and make a decision.

Quote #9

"Put all excuses aside and remember this; you are capable."

- Zig Ziglar (67 Quotes About Overcoming Adversity and Challenges in Your Life, 2019).

How many excuses have you created throughout your life to explain why you can't do something? I bet the number is uncountable. Don't worry. You aren't alone. We all love excuses. They are our go-to response for anything that incites fear within us or for when we simply don't want to. However, how many times are you going to let your excuses hold you back or make you incapable of finishing a task? At what point do your excuses stop becoming excuses and start becoming a crutch? You cannot let the fear of failure serve as an excuse for not trying. You want to know why? Because you are capable of handling anything that life throws at you. Yes. You are one hundred percent capable of handling the issues in your life — it has simply become too easy to create an excuse to avoid dealing with the problem.

How many obstacles have you tackled before in the past and won? More than you can count I am sure. So, why do you let your fear hold you back from challenges that you have never encountered before? Your self-doubt is something that starts deep within you and that no one else can change for you. You are the person responsible for holding yourself back.

I find it helpful during times of self-doubt to sit down and write a list of all of my accomplishments. Both big and small — trust me, those small ones count too. Any accomplishment, even those that you think might not be worthy of making it on the list, should go down too. Write it down. You need to. It will be the entire difference in how you perceive yourself. Once you have your list of accomplishments written down, take some time and reflect on how you felt before you accomplished each task. Were you afraid? Were you nervous? Were you doubting your capabilities?

Then reflect on how you managed to accomplish the obstacle despite your nervousness about your abilities to handle the issue. You did it! With help or on your own, it doesn't matter. The point is that you proved you were capable. So, what is different with this challenge? Nothing! Remind yourself of this when you try and create excuses and reasons for why you can't. Better yet, always combat each excuse with a reason why you can! This balances out the battlefield and leaves you with a positive outlook on why you are capable of tackling the issue ahead of you.

Quote #10

"Accept the challenges so that you can feel the exhilaration of victory."
- *George S. Patton (67 Quotes About Overcoming Adversity and Challenges in Your Life, 2019).*

Do you find yourself rejecting challenges because "they are too hard?" What happens when you reject a challenge? You automatically fail before you have even started. You give yourself no room to prove that small negative voice in your head wrong.

I want to challenge you to start accepting challenges and adversity into your life rather than avoiding them. Embrace the uncertainty that adversity brings because when you do this then you allow yourself a chance to feel what it means to win. It is difficult to try and start accepting issues that you have spent your whole life running away from. I understand that. I used to be in your shoes too! If the problem scared me, I put on my running shoes and I ran as far away as I could. However, this only served as a crutch to me later on in life and I found that I had never learned to deal with adversity, only how to run from it.

When we escape the issues in our life in this way, we are creating a handicap for ourselves that we are entirely at fault for. No one wants to be incapable of handling their own issues. And the sense of victory that a person feels when they manage to see the other side of the mountain they are battling, is one that everyone should feel in their lifetime. I am not saying start tackling every problem in your life. This is a lifetime issue that you have created by running away from your problems, so you will need to take it one step at a time to repair.

Baby steps are the first thing you should do when you decide to start accepting your adversity. This means accept the small challenges first. Don't bite off more than you can chew. If you start out small you can slowly expand until you feel confident in tackling the bigger issues in your life. Don't worry about how long they've been there for. When you are done tackling the smaller issues, the big ones will still be there waiting patiently for you. Use the exhilaration that you feel from completing each task to propel you onto the next one. This can help ensure that you remain positive about what you are asking yourself to do with each challenge. For example, maybe you have a fractious relationship with both of your parents, and you have always run away from repairing it. A baby step might be offering an olive branch to the parent who is most likely to accept it. You want to slowly approach fixing this relationship with the first parent and take every interaction as a small challenge. Use the victories from your successful interactions to propel you into initiating more interactions. When you have finally smoothed the bridge with the one parent use that new relationship and the feelings of success to initiate the first steps toward broaching the more challenging parent.

That is only one example of a way you can create smaller challenges to give you smaller victories that help propel you to the final victory you are looking for. There are many ways that you can start implementing this change in your life, you simply have to be aware of where it is easiest for you to create this change. For example, is there a small issue in your work life or personal life that you can create small steps leading towards a bigger end goal? This can help you journey toward your victory as well as change your mind set about how you have handled adversity in the past.

All you need to do is allow yourself to be accepting that adversity is a part of this life and that sometimes you need to face it head on. When you do this, then and only then, can you begin to understand the exhilaration your success can bring you.

- -

Chapter 3: Overcoming Fear

Quote #1

"He who is not every day conquering some fear has not learned the secret to life."

- *Ralph Waldo Emerson (Edberg, 2019).*

Fear is a natural part of this world. There are moments throughout our lifetime where we might feel paralyzed by an intense fear. There are also small moments every day where we might feel a pinprick of fear here and there. Sometimes we ignore these fears, or we try and put them off to be dealt with later. In certain situations, these fears can prove to be hazardous as they prevent us from excelling both personally and professionally.

In the words of Emerson, there is a fear that we should be conquering every day. It does not have to be a new fear every day, but simply a fear that we are steadfastly working toward solving or overcoming. You see, when we see through our fears we are constantly moving forward through life and evolving. However, when we allow our fears to take control, then we stay stagnant and we end up in the same place we will always be.

Life will never be easy all the time. Life will never always let you skate on by with no cares. You need to accept that fact to be able to move forward with facing your fears. Conquering those pinprick fears that tickle down your spine is one of the best ways to not only adapt, learn, and evolve but also to discover how life truly works!

So, why do we let fear paralyze us? I am sure that at some point in your life you experienced the paralyzing sensation of being so afraid of a situation that you could not move even if you wanted to. This is not a unique experience to you alone, even if it does feel like this at the time. When we first encounter something that spikes fear within us, we want to run away from the fear-inducing trigger, and we tell ourselves "I can't do this."

Sometimes, all we are afraid of is failing. We don't want to lose what we are doing or what we have gained so far in life and it can become very traumatic to contemplate the loss of our accomplishments. There are even times where we might feel like one failure will negate all the success we have encountered up until this point. The fear of failing will prevent you from doing anything that might benefit you. And while you initially might think it is all in your head, take a moment and examine how you feel when you are experiencing this fear. You do physically feel fear manifest in your body. The place it normally blossoms will be in your gut. It feels heavy and then you start feeling nervous.

Fear occurs on different gradients and every trigger affects each person differently. You might feel your mouth go dry or your throat constrict at the thought of confronting your fear. Your heart might begin to pound which in turn makes your pulse race. There are a lot of physical indicators of fear and these are more often than not the deciding factors that make our minds turn away from the fear.

When you are working to overcome fear, you need to understand that it is okay to be afraid. In fact, it is perfectly normal to experience fear. Everyone experiences fear and if they tell you that they don't, then they are only afraid of confronting their fears. Start tackling your smaller fears. Allow yourself to take stock in your physical feelings and then ask yourself what you are really afraid of. Once you can put the fear into perspective for yourself, then you make it easier to overcome.

Quote #2

"Do the thing you fear and continue to do so. This is the quickest and surest way of all victory over fear."

- Dale Carnegie (Edberg, 2019).

With those fears that crop up every day it can be hard to convince yourself to keep going back and conquering them. I know, I know. I am telling you to keep walking back into the very event that is inducing anxiety for you. It is not a pleasant feeling; however, it has long-term benefits that you don't want to lose.

When you continue to confront your fears daily, you find that you will soon have victory over them. In fact, one day you might wake up and realize that your stomach doesn't constrict at the thought of confronting what used to strike fear into you. No longer is your mouth dry or your pulse racing. You simply no longer fear the object or task that used to cause you stress. That is a pretty great feeling and I am speaking from experience.

Facing your fears is a tough experience that elicits the fight or flight response, causing us to run away. It takes time to build up the courage to face your fears, so don't expect to do so overnight. Fortunately, there are techniques to help you build up your courage to face your fears.

You can start by visualizing yourself performing with confidence and competence in an area where you are fearful. Your subconscious mind will accept your visual image as instructions for your performance, giving you the courage to face your fears. Through visualizing, your self-image is altered, making you believe you will succeed in your task. For example, you have a fear of public speaking and need to give a speech in front of your class. To perform well on your speech, you visualize your classmates enjoying your speech. They give you a standing ovation at the end and your teacher praises your public speaking skills. When it's your turn to speak, you walk up to the front of the classroom with confidence and receive an A on your assignment.

Quote #3

"He who has overcome his fears will truly be free."

- *Aristotle.*

Fear is one of the strongest human emotions that holds us back. Take a minute to think about a time that you felt afraid to perform a task. Did you give an excuse to get out of doing the task? When people are afraid, they tend to ignore the situation or find a way to excuse themselves from the task. For instance, right before it's your turn to go up to the board and perform a math exercise, you excuse yourself to use the bathroom. This is an example of fear denying your true freedom.

Fear gives you limits. When you overcome these limits, you will realize your true capabilities.

You won't be afraid to take the next step to get the promotion, dream job, build a house, or start a business. Overcoming your fear means you remove the limits placed on yourself.

One factor about fear is it can keep you from believing in yourself. When you believe you can't reach a goal, you won't try. For example, Bill has always wanted to open a bookstore. Since high school, he's worked in bookstores and knows this is what he wants to do. But he fears failure and believes his bookstore won't be successful. Bill's fear keeps him from following his dream.

When you feel fear, your anxiety can increase. Anxiety makes you worry about the future and think the worst possible outcome. For Bill, he sees his bookstore going out of business and he feels the loss of losing his dream. Therefore, Bill allows his fear to keep him in a cage.

To overcome your fear, you need to acknowledge your fear and change your negative thoughts to positive ones. For example, Bill will imagine himself operating a successful bookstore. Another way is to practice mindful meditation by focusing on your breathing. You will close your eyes and start with regular breaths. Focus on your breath as you inhale and exhale. You can even imagine fear leaving your body as you exhale and breathing courage into your body as you inhale. After a few regular breaths, you will focus on deep and slow breaths. This type of breathing puts your body into a naturally relaxed state, making it easier for you to remain mindful of your thoughts and actions.

Quote #4

"Fear comes from uncertainty. When we are absolutely certain, whether of our worth or worthlessness, we are almost impervious to fear."
- *William Congreve (Sweatt, 2016).*

One of the biggest reasons we feel fear is because we don't know what is going to happen in the future. We will worry about anything that can happen. This feeling often escalates for people who are overwhelmed with emotions, stressed, or struggle with mental illness, such as anxiety. People feel that they must know what is going to happen so they can prepare themselves. But, because we can't know for certain, we prepare ourselves for the worst possible outcome. This feeds our fears, causing us to become overwhelmed by our unknowing future.

Take a moment to think about when you felt fear over your future and when you didn't. When you felt fear, you may have noticed your heart racing, heavy breathing, or panic setting in. You may have started to put yourself down by telling yourself you didn't try hard enough or you didn't do well. Chances are, when you didn't feel fear, you knew what was about to happen or you had a pretty good idea. You may have been through the situation before, or you were warned about the situation. Whatever it is, you could prepare, allowing you to let go of your fear and focus on the task at hand.

While fear creates challenges in your life, it also holds many benefits once you overcome it. You will develop a strong force within you that allows you to convert your fear into courage. Once you reach this stage of fear, you will start to live a fulfilling life. You won't be afraid of what is ahead. Instead, you will move forward with your head held high and the knowledge that you can achieve your dreams.

There are five main steps you need to incorporate in your life when you feel fear. These steps are important when it comes to overcoming every negative emotion. Therefore, you can use these steps whenever you have challenges within your emotions, such as guilt and anger.

Accept the fear. No matter how strong you feel you are, your fear will never go away. Everyone can feel fear and allow it to control the way they think, act, and speak. There is nothing you can do to completely erase fear that you feel. This is a fact that you need to accept. You should also accept your feelings of fear when they arise, whether you are driving down the street or a police officer is walking up to your door. Accepting fear will allow you to control the emotion and deal with the task at hand in a logical way.

Identify your fear. Take time to ask yourself, "Why am I feeling this way?" Don't worry about what answer jumps into your head. You need to be honest with yourself in order to advance. You might find that you feel frightened because of a childhood memory or due to your struggles with anxiety. Identifying the reason, you feel afraid will help you learn to deal with your fears because you will see it as an opportunity to work toward fulfilling your lifestyle.

Feel your fear. Accepting and identifying the reason you're afraid can cause people to push everything aside. It can make you want to ignore your fear and focus on something else. This is one of the biggest mistakes you can make. You need to allow yourself to feel afraid so you can work on decreasing your fears. If you ignore them, they are going to increase.

Face your fears. You have probably heard this saying many times within your life. You need to face your fears in order to overcome them and it's true. We fear what is going to happen if we quit our comfortable job with benefits and start our own business, which is a dream. When you feel afraid, it's often the best time to move forward.

Practice facing your fears. Even if you overcome your current fears, more fears are going to show themselves. They are going to try to bring you back down. Don't allow this to happen. Start practicing this step-by-step process every time you feel afraid. Think of facing your fears as a skill, so you can gain better control of your emotions and reach your highest potential.

Quote #5

"One of the greatest discoveries a man makes, one of his great surprises, is to find he can do what he was afraid he couldn't do."
- *Henry Ford (Sweatt, 2016).*

No matter how confident you are, there are times that you worry you can't accomplish a task. It doesn't matter what the task is, what matters is that you are convinced that you can't do it. This belief leads to fear, one of the strongest emotions that can take over your mind. Once you start to believe that you can't do something, you will start to see a domino effect in your life. There is always more that you fear you can't accomplish.

But what makes you think you can't accomplish the task? Did you try before and make a mistake? Is this new territory and you're not sure how to go about the job? Whatever it is that makes you afraid to do something, you need to acknowledge and accept it. You need to work through this fear as you are going to find yourself surprised at the other end.

This is exactly what Henry Ford talked about in his quote. People fear what they don't know they can do. However, once they overcome this fear and complete their task, even if they make a mistake along the way, they are amazed by what they can accomplish.

There are many ways that you can overcome your fears and show yourself what you are made of. How you handle this step in your path of fulfillment depends on your personality. For example, some people are going to face the challenge head-on. They will get the task and find a way to complete it. Other people need more coaching. This coaching doesn't necessarily come from others, it comes from inside themselves. They need time to tell themselves they are successful, hard-working, and can complete the task.

The more you discover your capabilities, the easier this process will become. Once you see that you can achieve something you didn't believe you could, you will ask yourself, "What else can I do?" You will find the strength to acknowledge and push through your fears to complete another task. Over time, you will find your fears subside as you take on one challenge after another. The power you will feel within yourself is one of the greatest strengths in your life. It doesn't matter how much you can physically carry, when it comes to your emotional strength, you can take on the world.

All you need to do is follow the old phrase, "put one foot in front of the other." Know what your goal is and work to accomplish this goal. Remember, every goal has a series of smaller steps you need to complete to reach your main goal. Focus on the series of smaller steps, one by one, and not specifically on your goal. Reward yourself for each small step you take to reach your bigger goal. Of course, you don't want to forget to reward yourself once you reach your goal as well.

Quote #6

"I have learned over the years that when one's mind is made up, this diminishes fear; knowing what must be done does away with fear."

- *Rosa Parks (Sweatt, 2016).*

Years after Rosa Parks refused to get up on the city bus, she gave an interview about the incident. When asked what went through her mind when she refused to move to the back of the bus, she simply stated that she was tired. Parks was tired from working at her job. Of course, she was tired of the racism and segregation she faced throughout her life, but she never went on that bus to protest against segregation. She went on that bus so she could get home and rest after working another 12-hour day.

Rosa Parks didn't focus on her fear when she told the bus driver "no" she would not move to the back of the bus. She focused on what she felt was right. As she said in her quote, she made up her mind and decided to take a stand, even if it was simply because she was tired. The process of making up your mind doesn't always happen as quickly as it did for Rosa Parks that day on the bus. Parks only had mere seconds to decide what she was going to do. Even after the bus driver repeatedly demanded she moved to the back, she kept her ground and refused - because she had made up her mind.

No matter how long it takes you to make up your mind over a decision, focus on Parks as she can give you the inspiration you need to begin your process. Once you start to make up your mind, stand your ground, and realize what has to get done, you will find your fear washing away.

You will start to make decisions easily and come to realize your true capabilities. You won't feel the need to ask people - or yourself - if you are making the right decision because you will know you are.

Fear is one of the strongest emotions people feel. It's a negative emotion that will only bring out more negativity within your life. When you make up your mind to overcome your fears and focus on the jobs you need to acquire, you will find yourself focusing on the positives. The belief that you can accomplish what you set your mind to blossoms and you reach a higher level of yourself. In other words, you are one step closer to your best self.

Quote #7

"If you look into your own heart, and you find nothing wrong there, what is there to worry about? What is there to fear?"

- *Confucius*.

There are many events that we fear in our lives. You might be out in the woods and fear that you just heard a bear. Your mind racing as you think, "What do I do if I see the bear?" You might feel fear when you are starting a new job, "What if they don't like me? What if I make a mistake? Am I wearing the right clothes to make a good impression?" You may feel fear when your supervisor asks to speak with you. Your spins from everything you have done, how well you have performed your duties, and everything you haven't gotten completed.

If you allow yourself to feel fear and worry, there are tons of factors within your life you can fear. However, the key is you need to allow this fear to come through. You let the worry, which turns into fear, overtake your emotions. Soon, all you can do is think of your fears and the worst-case scenario. After all, because your supervisor called you into their office means you've done something wrong, correct? Nope - it simply means that your supervisor has something they want to tell or ask you.

Confucius brings up the point that we often fear the little things. While you might feel that fearing about the smaller events in life is better than the larger ones, the truth is, the little fear turns into a large fear. Fear is like a snowball rolling down the hill. It is going to start out small, but as it collects other pieces, it is going to grow.

To get this snowball to crash into a tree and

break apart, Confucius says you need to look within your heart to let go of your fear. You need to ask yourself, "Did I do my best?" and when you answer, "Yes, I did" you can let that fear break apart. One way to do this is by understanding that life is full of surprising situations. You can never prepare for everything life is going to throw at you. However, you can prepare to overcome your fear and face the situation head-on. You can decide that worrying about the situation is not going to help you in the bigger picture. In fact, it won't help you in the smaller picture either.

You need to realize that life happens and there is nothing you can do to change this. There will be times that you plan everything out for your day only to find that you've completed nothing on your list because life took you in another direction. This is frustrating, but it isn't worth stressing over. Let it go and remember tomorrow is a new day.

If you planned a birthday party for your child only to forget to pick up the cake, look within yourself and realize that you did your best. You planned a whole birthday party for your toddler by yourself and people had a great time. You managed to call your friend in time, who picked up the cake and made it before people started eating. Instead of focusing on forgetting the cake, you need to let it go because you did your best, and everything worked out in the end. To incorporate this quote into your life, you need to think "I have done my best to prepare. What happens, happens. I will accept it and be proud of my work because I did my best." Don't worry about the mistakes along the way or if you didn't perform as well as you wanted to. Focus on the fact that you did your best.

Quote #8

"Thinking will not overcome fear but action will."

- *W. Clement Stone (Scott, 2017).*

How often do you sit down to think about all the mistakes you made? If you are like most people, you will think of mistakes you made years ago. This can happen randomly throughout your day. You are driving to work and think about something you said to your significant other five years ago that hurt them. You fear that they still remember and will never forgive you for hurting them so much. You fear that your relationship is still not the same as it once was.

But what are you doing to make your relationship better? One statement is not going to damage your relationship to the point of no repair. It is a series of events that damages a relationship. You can say something bad or make a mistake and repair your relationship through your actions. Whether you fear for your relationship or your job - actions are always going to speak louder than words.

For example, your work performance has not been the strongest lately. You haven't been feeling well and you know this is affecting the way you work. You don't make your deadlines and you don't communicate with your boss like you used to. You know your boss is noticing your poor behavior, but you don't open up and talk to them about it because you fear for your job. You fear that your boss won't think you are as strong as they believe. You fear that they will think you are weak and unworthy of working for them. You can continue to worry about your work performance, or you can do what you need to do to change your performance.

You won't change your performance in a few days. In fact, it might even take more than a couple of months. However, the more you work toward taking the steps to make yourself feel healthy and change your work performance, the stronger you will become. This strength will allow you to face your fears, act on them, and overcome them. You will no longer think and worry about what could happen. Instead, you will focus on what will happen because you are working toward a goal and not just thinking about it.

The steps you take to act instead of think are going to depend on your situation. You may need to look beyond your current resources and get help from someone else. You may need to simply change your mindset. You may also need to see a doctor who can help you understand why you are so tired all the time. Whatever you need to do to overcome your fear, you need to act on it. This is the only true way that you can work to overcome your fear.

One of the ways you can focus on action is by writing what you want to accomplish. On the top of the paper, write your main goal. For example, you could write "improve my work performance." Then, you want to write down the steps you will take to accomplish this goal. Your steps may include:

- *Get more sleep.*
- *Visit the doctor.*
- *Eat healthier.*
- *Meditate every morning.*
- *Focus on positive thoughts.*
- *Improve my concentration.*

You can place as much detail in your steps as you want to. The key is to make sure you understand what the steps mean to help you accomplish your goal.

Quote #9

"Living with fear stops us taking risks, and if you don't go out on the branch, you're never going to get the best fruit."
- *Sarah Parish (Sweatt, 2016).*

In this quote, Sarah Parish is talking about our comfort zone. People don't like to step out of their comfort zone because of fear. Your comfort zone is anything from your current job to your home. For example, you've been in your position for five years. You do well in your job and always go above and beyond to help your co-workers. You've proven that you can not only handle your job, but receive a promotion, giving you more responsibility and supervision duties. When your supervisor tells you about your chance to move into the next position, you become frightened. You have never supervised another employee and your new role would give you more responsibilities. You feel comfortable in your current position and don't want to step into a new role to find out you can't perform your new duties. Therefore, you are faced with a decision: Do you take the new position and do your best, or do you stay in your current position because you are comfortable?

To understand what you are truly capable of, you need to branch out of your comfort zone and try something new. You never know what you are missing until you reach something new. The problem is, fear is going to stop you dead in your tracks when it comes to leaving your comfort zone. It's like this little tiny person is standing on your shoulder and telling you everything that could go wrong. It tells you that you don't know if you can handle the new responsibilities. You wonder what is going to happen if you fail in your new role.

To overcome your fear and take a step out of your comfort zone, you need to push that little person down and face your new adventure with your head held high. You need to tell your fears that you are capable of accomplishing anything you set your mind to. Sometimes, people will not think, they will just do. They will take a moment, step out of their comfort zone, and tell their supervisor, "I will take that position. Thank you for the opportunity."

The way you handle stepping out of your comfort zone depends on your personality. Some people are good with facing situations and other people need a little more time. They need to build up to their moment. No matter how you handle the situation, the goal is to take a step out of your comfort zone. You don't need to take a large step; you can take a baby step. You can take a step and go back into your comfort zone a couple of minutes later. Whatever process you feel you need to follow is what you need to do. However, you can't let your fear keep you in your comfort zone. This is allowing your fear to control your actions. One of the key steps in fulfilling your life is to control your emotions. It is only at this moment; you will reach the best fruit.

Quote #10

"Being aware of your fear is smart. Overcoming it is the mark of a successful person."

- *Seth Godin.*

By now you are aware that fear is a strong emotion. Seth Godin says it is smart to be aware. However, you need to move past that awareness and work toward overcoming your fear in order to reach your full potential - or as Godin says - become a successful person.

When you are aware of something, whether it is the way someone acts or an emotion, you simply know it exists. It doesn't mean that you take action and try to change the way someone treats you or learn how to handle your emotions. At the same time, you can't ignore the fact that you know fear exists. This is an important step to improving your life and the world around you. Realizing an emotion can take over your thought process and cause you to act in a certain way does show intelligence. But it doesn't show that you can reach the success you are capable of.

It's hard to talk about becoming a successful person without acknowledging that many people see success differently. Truthfully, some people might find this quote a little offensive at first. They might feel they are successful but know that they also let fear take control of their life from time to time. Letting fear get the best of you doesn't mean you aren't a successful person. If you feel successful, that is wonderful. That's an important belief to hold in your life. At the same time, you haven't reached your full success. You have only hit a comfortable level of your success. It's time to work toward your ultimate success.

There are many ways to overcome fear. You can use any of the techniques already discussed, or you can find different strategies. Sometimes, you need to find a strategy that matches with your current fear. When this happens, you need to ask yourself "What am I fearing?" and "Why do I feel this fear?" You need to dig deep and be honest with yourself. Sometimes you aren't going to like the answer you give yourself, but it is essential so you can move to the next step.

First, you need to remember it is always okay to feel fear. This chapter isn't here to tell that you shouldn't ever feel fear. Fear is a natural emotion that is healthy to feel from time to time. It can help you make the right decision, so you don't hurt yourself. However, it can also keep you from reaching a fulfilling life. That is the challenge of our negative emotions - they do come with their own pros and cons list.

Second, focus on taking small steps - you can even call them baby steps. You might stumble along the way like a toddler learning how to walk at first. But the more effort you put into overcoming your fear, the stronger your steps will become. The key is to not let fear paralyze you, which it has a habit of doing. Instead, you need to plan to take a small step every day. Take a moment every morning to think of something you are afraid of and make it a goal to overcome your fear by completing this action. For example, you are afraid of going to the gym during its busiest time. Therefore, you decide that you will do this today. You will walk into that gym with your head held high because there is nothing shameful about wanting and working to become healthier.

Third, talk to people who know you best. Your friends and family see talent inside of you that you don't see. They also see personality traits that you don't realize. They can help you overcome your fear by telling you what they feel you are capable of. Don't be modest when you talk to them. You can explain why you are asking them your questions, but then take their answers seriously. You will want to choose people whose opinion you value because you are more likely to listen to what they say. While you might not believe it at first, take time to think about it and remember, they are trying to help you. They are telling you what they truly see and believe.

- -

Chapter 4: Overcoming Loss

Quote #1

"Grief is not a disorder, a disease or a sign of weakness. It is an emotional, physical and spiritual necessity, the price you pay for love. The only cure for grief is to grieve."

- *Earl Grollman (20 Quotes About Grief, 2018).*

In the past, people believed showing signs of sadness or depression meant you were weak. It didn't matter what you were going through, whether it was the loss of a family member, friend, or home. What mattered is that you did everything you could to move on from the loss as quickly as possible. Of course, you were allowed to grieve, but you had to do so in the privacy of your home. Most people didn't want anyone else to know they were grieving. Fortunately, this isn't the popular way of thinking anymore, allowing people to openly grieve and receive support from their friends, family, and community that they need in order to pick up their pieces and carry one.

Human emotions are necessary. We need to feel our emotions, so we can learn and grow. Grief is an emotion we feel throughout our life, just as we do happiness. There is nothing wrong with feeling grief - no matter what you were taught growing up. Grief is not a sign of weakness; it does not say there is something mentally wrong with you. Grief is a sign of strength. It is a sign of compassion and care. It shows people that you are a person who loved someone. As Grollman states, grief is the "price you pay for love." (20 Quotes About Grief, 2018).

Grief is not an emotion that people want to feel. No one wants to feel the pain of losing someone they loved, their home, pets, or anything else. It's a pain that we often wish will go away quickly. Unfortunately, it's an emotional pain that we can't push away because it will hang on to us until we accept it, feel it, and grieve. If we allow grief to stay within us, we are causing more emotional pain and harming ourselves. We can find ourselves in a deep depression, unable to cope with life, quitting our job, and believing that we can't carry on without the person. Grief can become so powerful that it affects you physically. You may stop taking care of yourself. You won't focus on eating healthy and you will stop exercising. You will find yourself becoming physically ill. The ways that grief can affect you are truly amazing. This is one of the biggest reasons you need to work through your grief.

First, you need to understand that grieving is an individual experience. Everyone is going to handle their grief differently. Some people are going to talk openly about how they feel while other people are going to keep it inside longer. They will eventually talk about it, but they need a longer time to process grief internally. Other people will express their grief creatively through writing or painting. There are also people who become angry and will find themselves lashing out.

Second, it's important to realize that the grieving process takes time. Grief isn't an emotion you can "fix" in a couple of hours or even a couple of weeks. It can take months and even a year or so to fully get over the loss of something, a divorce, or losing your dream job. You need to acknowledge the grieving process and allow your emotions to flow. The key is to be patient with yourself and your grieving process. You don't want to force yourself to "get over it" as this will only deepen your emotional wounds.

Fortunately, there are a lot of ways that will allow you to cope with your grieving process.

Seek support from other people. You don't need to grieve alone. You might find support in your friends and family or you may need to look to seeing a therapist. No matter where you go for support, you need to seek people who care about you and want to help you through this difficult time.

It is important to understand the difference between grief and depression. Some people will sink into a depression during the grieving process. It's essential that you understand depression, so you know when you need to seek help or any sort of treatment.

Don't stop taking care of yourself physically. One way that you can support your emotional health is by taking care of your physical health. Keep your daily routine, exercise, continue to eat healthy, take your vitamins, and get enough sleep.

Understand that you might start to feel emotions that you haven't felt before. You also might show behaviors you usually don't exhibit. This is part of the grieving process. However, you always need to keep your safety and the safety of other people in mind. If you find yourself acting out in a dangerous way or having negative thoughts, seek the help you need.

Quote #2

"The reality is that you will grieve forever. You will not 'get over' the loss of a loved one; you will learn to live with it. You will heal and you will rebuild yourself around the loss you have suffered. You will be whole again, but you will never be the same. Nor should you be the same nor would you want to."

- *Elisabeth Kubler-Ross (Sedulia, 2013).*

Elisabeth Kubler-Ross is a psychiatrist who introduced the five stages of grief in 1969. While people have since adjusted or established their own stages, the five stages remain the main stages of grief. They are as follows:

1. Denial - You don't believe this is happening.

2. Anger - You want to find someone to blame

because you don't understand why this is happening.

3. Bargaining - This is often the stage where people try to make a plea to God, they might say something like, "If you bring them back, I will give you...."

4. Depression - You feel too sad to do anything. Some people struggle to get out of bed.

5. Acceptance. You find peace with your loss and focus on picking up the pieces of your life.

Kubler-Ross spent a lot of time focusing on grief and trying to help people understand the process of grief. She wanted people to understand that grief isn't something you will get over. It isn't something that you can move from quickly. In fact, you won't truly get over the loss of a loved one. You will always miss them. You will always feel like there is a hole in your heart from where they once were. Even though you still have memories of them, and even some of their possessions, you miss their voice, hugs, kisses, and smell. You miss their presence. This is part of the grief that you always have. Always having a part of grief with you doesn't mean you won't pick up the pieces of your life and create a new normal. It simply means that you will always miss them. One factor to realizing is there is nothing wrong with missing someone. Even if you lost someone 30 years ago, you can still miss them every day. Take your time to remember some of the good times you shared together. Take a moment to call someone and talk about the person you miss. You can write the memories down or share them with your children or your grandchildren. Accept that you miss them and help yourself work through the moment.

Don't believe that you have to be the person you were before you suffered the loss. You are going to change, and this isn't a bad change. If you were the same person as before, it would show that you didn't truly love the person; that they didn't make an impact on your life. Allow yourself to change and grow with the loss. You might have moments where you don't recognize yourself, but this is just a part of loss. As time goes on, you will overcome your biggest struggles when it comes to change and start to reach your new best self.

Quote #3

"What we once enjoyed and deeply loved we can never lose, for all that we love deeply becomes a part of us."

- Helen Keller (20 Quotes About Grief, 2018).

When we spend time with people, they become a part of us. They are a part of our heart and soul. We hold on to their memories as they bring us laughter and joy. You hold on to the words they spoke to us because they helped us learn and grow. These are factors that we don't lose when the person dies. These are the pieces of their life - our lives together - that we hold dearly.

Helen Keller tried to help people understand loss by telling them the person is only physically gone. There is a part of them that is still with us and we can hold this part of them for the rest of our lives. No matter who you lost, whether it is a spouse, parent, sibling, friend, or pet, part of them will always be with your internally. Therefore, the person is never truly gone.

This can help you when it comes to grieving the loss of a loved one. Instead of holding your memories and love for them internally, you can spread the memories and love. You can do this creatively through writing, drawing, or singing. You can also focus on talking about the person and what they did for you. Tell people why they are such an important part of your life. Talk about the memories you shared and how they helped you become the person you are today. Treat the memories and love you still hold from this person like the warmth you feel from the sunlight. Allow this warmth to take over your heart and soul. Smile as you feel their warmth and look up to the sky. Believe that they are looking down and smiling with you.

Above all, never feel that you lose the pieces of yourself the person gave you. If you need to, write down everything you feel they gave you and reflect on what you wrote. Acknowledge the emotions that flow through you, even if you feel they are like a raging river. It is all part of the grieving process and you are allowing yourself to heal a little more.

Quote #4

"You cannot die of grief, though it feels as if you can. A heart does not actually break, though sometimes your chest aches as if it is breaking. Grief dims with time. It is the way of things. There comes a day when you smile again, and you feel like a traitor. How dare I feel happy. How dare I be glad in a world where my father is no more. And then you cry fresh tears, because you do not miss him as much as you once did and giving up your grief is another kind of death."

- Laurell K. Hamilton (20 Quotes About Grief, 2018).

Laurell K. Hamilton's quote is filled with some of the most powerful words when it comes to grief. They are all true. You are going to feel like grief will lead you to your own death because you don't know how you will continue life without the person. You feel that your heart is broken, when it isn't physically possible for your heart to break. But this doesn't mean that it isn't a part of grief.

Over time, you will start to put the pieces of your life back together. You will pick up these shattered pieces one by one and place them back into your puzzle of life. Sometimes, you will find these pieces fall out again, but you will pick them back up and carry on. Soon, you will find yourself enjoying parts of life again. You will laugh when your dog does something silly or smile when you talk to someone. You will start to feel happy - and then you will think about the person who you lost and wonder how you can act this way. How can you be happy when you are supposed to be grieving?

Just as the love and memories you have for the person will never leave you, there will always be a part of grief inside of you. This is the part that makes you miss the person, even 20 years after their passing. This is the part of grief that makes you focus on the memories and love. Just because you don't think of the person every second of every day, doesn't mean you love and miss them any less. It means you are doing exactly what you are supposed to, and what they would want you to do - you are moving on. You are re-developing your life and they are extremely proud and happy that you are doing so.

The part of grief where you realize that you are carrying on is acceptance and it is an important part of the grieving process. You need to keep in mind that this doesn't mean you are forgetting about the person, even if you feel you don't remember their smell. You still remember everything about the person that you did during your first stages of grief. When you come to this part in your grief process, you need to allow your feelings to come as they are. Don't feel that you need to push certain feelings aside or you should feel a certain way. The way you feel is how you are handling the grief process.

Quote #5

"Perhaps they are not the stars in the sky, but rather openings where our loved ones shine down to let us know they are happy."
- *Unknown (Zwarensteyn, 2018).*

Children who go through the death of a family member or friend are often told that their soul heads into the afterworld and they become a star. You can even go online and honor someone you have lost with a star. You can choose the star and you receive a document stating that this specific star is named after the person.

The above quote takes this a bit farther. Instead of saying the person become a star, it says that the stars are how we know they are happy. It's how we can look up and know that they are doing well, smiling down at us and proud of who we are. Believing that stars are a doorway to communication with the people we have lost in our life, can help us overcome our challenges with grief. This allows us to look up toward the stars and know that they are no longer in pain, they no longer feel the stress of life, they are happy, and they want us to find our happiness, too.

It isn't always easy to get an adult to feel this way. People often feel that if they believe something like this, it is silly because they are "too old." They should know how to handle their emotions and grief without feeling they have to look up at the stars. But, looking up at the stars shining down on you can give you a sense of peace in your grief.

You don't need to share the moment you look up at the stars and believe it is a form of communication from your loved on. You don't need to stop and focus on a certain star. You can look out your window and notice the stars shining, blinking, and giving off various colors. Take in the emotions you feel when you notice the stars, even if it is for a brief moment.

Quote #6

"Grief falls upon human beings as the rain, not selecting good or evil, visiting the innocent, condemning those who have done no wrong."

- *Richard Jefferies.*

There is a popular phrase that states, "the good die young." This is part of what Jefferies is talking about in the above quote. But he takes it a step further and states that it doesn't matter who the person is, what they did in life, or even how old they are - death can take them home.

We know that death can come at any time and any age, it is just a fact of life that people don't like to talk about. Instead, we like to create the illusion that people will only die if they have lived a good and long life. We like to imagine that people who bring evil into the world are going to pass on before people who spend their life helping others. Unfortunately, this is not how it happens. Sometimes we lose a child and sometimes a young child loses a parent.

Death is hard to process when someone passes away at 100 years old. It's no secret that death can be harder to process when someone dies at the age of 10. People who die young will often make us wonder why someone so young and innocent was taken from us. Why can't everyone go on to live until they are 100 years old?

These questions can be hard for us to accept, partially because we can never receive a true answer. These questions are going to bring a lot of emotions, some that we will struggle to overcome. The key is to have patience. Whenever you are dealing with grief, you need to accept how you feel and give yourself time to overcome grief.

No matter when a person passes away, you are going to go through the same stages of grief. It's true that some death will be harder to process than others. You will have a tougher time getting over some. There will be times where you spend years trying to process your grief. The level of grief we feel does depend on how we lost the person and how important they are to us.

Quote #7

"Your grief path is yours alone, and no one else can walk it, and no one else can understand it."

- *Terri Irwin.*

Terri Irwin is one of the many people who had to grieve publicly when she lost her husband, Steve Irwin. Many people believe that those who carry a celebrity status and grieve in the public eye are surrounded by people who understand and support them. While there are usually hundreds, if not thousands to millions, of people sending their support, it doesn't mean that the person receiving the support feels any differently. Furthermore, no one should feel that people who have to grieve in the public eye are going to process their grief differently.

When you are dealing with grief, no matter who it is or how much support you have around you, it is still going to be your grief. While you go through the same stages everyone else does, the path that you take is your path. No one else is on this path and no one else is going to join you on this path. Everyone else is on their own path of grieving. It's okay to feel alone when you are on your path because only you can understand it.

Many people believe that they need to be surrounded by friends and family in times of grief. While it will help, you also need to spend time alone. You need to reflect on your emotions and your path of grief. You need to allow yourself to accept what you are going through, where you are in the grieving process, and understand that you can work on healing yourself by yourself. In fact, some people heal easier when they are allowed to be alone with their emotions.

Processing your emotions in your time and in your way is going to help you continue walking on your path.

If you need to be alone to grieve, it is okay to ask people to leave. Of course, they are going to be worried about you because they care about and love you. People feel a need to comfort others in times of need. It's hard for people to back away and allow you to process your grief alone. But, if you feel this is truly what you need to do, then you need to be open and take some "me" time.

Quote #8

"When someone you love dies, and you're not expecting it, you don't lose her all at once; you lose her in pieces over a long time — the way the mail stops coming, and her scent fades from the pillows and even from the clothes in her closet and drawers. Gradually, you accumulate the parts of her that are gone. Just when the day comes — when there's a particular missing part that overwhelms you with the feeling that she's gone, forever — there comes another day, and another specifically missing part."

- *John Irving (Mort, 2015).*

There is a difference with grief when it comes to losing someone suddenly versus expecting it. While you will go through the same stages of grief, you will handle the grief process a bit differently - at least during certain parts. When you expect it, you can take the time to prepare. You can start to plan the service and you can even take the time to say your final goodbye. This won't make the grieving process easier, but it eases some of the questions. It also helps ease the shock of loss. This isn't saying you won't feel any shock and there is always a bit of shock that comes with hearing someone has passed on. But the shock won't cut you as deeply as a death you are not expecting.

When someone dies suddenly, you can't prepare for the loss or the shock. You don't know how you are going to react until you hear the person is gone. You might break down crying immediately or sit there in silence as you try to process the words you just heard. If you are in charge of the arrangements for the funeral, you need to do your best to work through your emotions and handle the process. It isn't easy, but it is necessary as one of the ways you will start to pick up the pieces is through the funeral.

A sudden death is going to leave you with situations that you did not plan. For example, you may need to call people to tell them the person passed away, this includes the Post Office as the person's mail will need to be sent back. It means that you need to stop their prescription medication, notify their policyholders, and follow any other steps that need to be taken. This isn't something that you will do in one day. In fact, it might take you a month or so. Furthermore, you won't even think of everything that you should have done. For example, you will receive a piece of their mail one day and realize you should have contacted that company. It's important to remember that when this happens, it's okay. You can't think clearly in times of grief.

Other than these factors, there are other situations that are going to arise, making you feel the loss all over again. It's going to happen when you realize that you need to pack up their belongings and give them to family or donate them. When you go to smell their jacket and realize the smell is fading. You will feel like you are losing the person all over again when you come across their journal or something of high importance to them - something you know they cherished. These moments will happen randomly. You can't always tell when they are going to come, but you should always allow yourself to accept your emotions and feel the grief.

Quote #9

"In this sad world of ours, sorrow comes to all. Perfect relief is not possible, except with time. You cannot now realize that you will ever feel better. And yet it is a mistake. You are sure to be happy again. To know this, which is certainly true, will make you some less miserable now. I have had experience enough to know what I say, and you need only to believe it to feel better at once."

- Abraham Lincoln (Raymond, 2019).

Most people know Abraham Lincoln as the 16th President of the United States, the one who ended slavery through the Civil War. What a lot of people don't know is that Lincoln's life was filled with grief that he never got over, because as we have learned, you never fully get over grief. At the age of 9, Lincoln's mother passed away. As a father, Lincoln lost two of his four sons. Lincoln remained open about his feelings of grief and knew that from the age of 9, he never got over his grief. In fact, Lincoln's grief led him down a road of depression through his adult life.

When Lincoln spoke these words, America was going through one of its darkest times. Lincoln wasn't the only person who struggled over all the loss the Civil War brought to the United States, the whole country mourned, and he understood this. Lincoln also understand that everyone needed their time to mourn and that people did not understand why their family member had to be taken during the time of war. This understanding came because Lincoln felt the same way, not only because losing thousands of soldiers, but because he never understood why his mother and children were taken from him.

At the same time, Lincoln understood the grieving process, even if people didn't understand it during his time. He knew that you do pick up the pieces of your life, one by one, and start to carry on. It's going to happen in different ways for everyone because we all react to death in a different way.

With this quote, Lincoln was trying to help people who were overcome with grief because of a loss they suffered during the Civil War. He tried to do what so many people try to do when you are grieving - help you through the process. The only difference is, Lincoln didn't try to do this for one person or a family, he tried to do it for the whole country. It's important to note that every word Lincoln said in his quote is true. You will start to heal over time. While you will always feel a sense of loss, you will start to find your happiness again. Lincoln also felt that people needed to know this because it would give them a little hope that one day, they would start to feel better. One day they would find their smile again and laugh. However, people would also continue to struggle as they remember the loss and share memories of the person. This is natural when it comes to losing someone you love. Hope is something that we should always have when it comes to tough times in our life. While we might not feel very hopeful in the moment, knowing that your days will get better as you begin to pick up the pieces of your life, gives you hope. This doesn't mean that you are working toward forgetting the person as you will never do that. It means that you are starting to create a new normal. One that will allow you to feel happy and full of life again.

Quote #10

"When those you love die, the best you can do is honor their spirit for as long as you live. You make a commitment that you're going to take whatever lesson that person or animal was trying to teach you, and you make it true in your own life. It's a positive way to keep their spirit alive in the world by keeping it alive in yourself."

- *Patrick Swayze (Raymond, 2019).*

From the moment people hear someone has passed on, they want to do whatever they can to remember the person. Just like people handle grief in different ways, people will handle this process in different ways. For example, some people will get together with friends and family and share their memories. Other people are going to keep to themselves and think of the memories. They might choose to write them down or write down something to honor the person. Some people are going to light candles and say a prayer. As time goes on, the way we honor the person is going to change. There will be times that people get together and share their stories, such as in a memorial service. Other times people will focus on their thoughts or spend their time talking to the person at their gravesite.

Soon, you find yourself thinking about everything the person taught you. If you are a child, you might focus on these teachings and make sure you follow them to the best of your abilities. This doesn't mean you won't make a mistake or forget something they taught you one night. But it does mean that you will try your best to follow their guidance and continue to make them proud. If you ever find yourself making a mistake, don't feel that your loved one is disappointed in you. Don't allow people to ask you "What would your mother say?" Instead, know that they still love you, are still proud of you, and learn from your mistakes.

One of the best ways to work through your grief is all the moments you spend remembering them and honoring their memory. This is why you should make a commitment to do what you can. Even if you only make it to the cemetery once a year to place flowers on their grave for Memorial Day, make it a day to honor them. Don't feel that you need to do something special in order to honor their memory. Whatever you feel will honor their memory is exactly what you need to do. For example, you might light a candle every year on the day they passed away. You might donate money in their honor to a local charity, or you might find yourself writing down memories and sharing them with pictures.

There is no right or wrong way to grieve or honor someone. You are going to go through the process that is best for you. You need to accept the process and handle it one step at a time. Don't rush through it because this will only make grieving worse. Be patient and understand that not everyone is going to understand the road you are on, but they are going to try. This is because they want to support you and help you through this process. Accept the help when you need, but don't feel that you always need to take their help. If you need to be alone, take time to be alone. Do what you feel is right in your heart as this is the true way that will allow your soul to slowly start healing from loss.

- -

Chapter 5: Finding Peace

Quote #1

"Love and peace of mind do protect us. They allow us to overcome the problems that life hands us. They teach us to survive... to live now... to have the courage to confront each day."

- Bernie Siegel.

No matter who you are, you will face struggles throughout your day. Some people are going to face tougher struggles than others. However, for each person their struggles are some of the most important events going on in their life. At the same time, struggles are known to break you down. They cause you to think negatively. For example, you might feel that you will not reach your level of success because of the struggles you have to overcome. You don't know how much more effort you can put forth everyday fighting a certain battle.

Struggles can make you feel lost. They can lead you to believe that people don't truly understand you, even when they say they do. They can make you think about all the mistakes you have made that led you down this path. You can feel cold and alone in the world, no matter who is with you or who says they are supporting you. This is something that is a natural feeling for many people, especially when they are overwhelmed by the challenges they face. Some people continuously repeat to themselves that God will only give them what they can handle. Other people don't believe in this. Not specifically because they don't believe in God, but because they believe they can't handle everything that life hands them. They feel like they are hanging by a thread and that this thread is about to break.

The moment you feel you have nothing left to give and that you can't handle any more obstacles, is the moment you need to turn your life toward faith. This isn't strictly faith in God, but faith in believing peace of mind will give you the strength to carry on. The strength is going to give you the courage you need to survive and continue giving your best every day.

It's not easy to reach this point and it is something that you will need to work on for a period of time. In fact, you will never stop working toward creating peace of mind. While you will reach a good level of peace, you need to make sure that you don't lose your peaceful mindset.

One of the best ways to reach peace is

through meditation. While not everyone will find meditation to be their way to a peaceful mind, most people believe in its magic. Another way to bring more peace into your life is to focus on essential oils and crystals. If you look into this path, you want to ensure you understand what the colors mean and focus on the ones you need to work on. You can also use various candles in order to give yourself a sense of peace.

The goal when it comes to developing your peace of mind is to focus on what you want to achieve. What is going to make you feel at peace? Do you need to have your dream job? Do you feel you need to create your own space in the house that describes who you are? You might feel you need to learn to cope with the stresses in your life because you are struggling to raise your family. Whatever your goals are, you need to be honest with yourself or you won't reach your peace of mind.

When it comes to a peaceful state of mind, it's important to realize this doesn't mean you won't feel overwhelmed or stressed from time to time. What it means is that you will find a way to handle the chaos in a peaceful way. You will turn to your strategies to help you maintain a peaceful mind and then take on the task at hand.

Quote #2

"Do not let the behavior of others destroy your inner peace."

- *Dalai Lama (Sweatt, 2016).*

When it comes to people who have found their inner peace, many people think about the Dalai Lama. He is a powerful figure that can help you overcome a lot of struggles in your life because he has found a version of his inner peace. Fortunately, he spends his time guiding other people who want to find their inner peace. One of the best quotes to help you is when he tells people to not let anyone destroy the inner peace you create.

We all know that this world is full of cruel people. There are people that pride themselves on bringing other people down. People who do this don't understand themselves and they don't have inner peace. They might feel that their world is crumbling and to make themselves feel better, they need to make you feel worse.

No matter how hard we try, it is hard to let go of the negative things people tell us. It's hard to forget about the names they call us or how they hurt us. However, it is essential if we want to continue working toward our inner peace. This isn't saying that you need to build a brick wall to protect yourself from the hateful things people say. You also should ignore people when they are being mean. Instead, you need to acknowledge them and treat them with kindness. This can be a difficult step to process because we feel the need to defend ourselves from people who are cruel. While there is never anything wrong with defending yourself, you also need to think about if it is necessary. You need to remember that the people who are hurting you are hurting themselves. If you truly want to find peace, you don't want to see other people hurting. You want to try to help them the best you can and sometimes this means giving them a smile when they try to push you down.

You will need to take time to refocus on your peace once you leave the negative situation. You might need to meditate or read a few uplifting quotes. You may find yourself on YouTube scrolling through motivational videos to find the best one to listen to. Some people will turn to their talent or skills to help them overcome the hurtful words the person said.

There are also times where you will feel a little down because of what other people have said. It is okay to feel this way, for a period of time. Don't let yourself be down for long. Do what you need to do to raise yourself back up and continue focusing on finding your peace. The key is to acknowledge the way the person made you feel. Don't ignore it or think that you shouldn't feel a certain way. There is never anything wrong with the way you feel. You feel a certain way because it's a part of who you are. Never feel ashamed for being who you are, especially when it deals with processing your emotions.

Quote #3

"You find peace not by rearranging the circumstances of your life, but by realizing who you are at the deepest level."

- *Eckhart Tolle (Sweatt, 2016).*

People often believe they are not at peace because of situations happening in their life. While stressful and chaotic events can cause you to lose sight of your peace, it doesn't mean that these situations are the reasons you don't feel peace. When someone reaches their inner peace, they are going to feel at peace through some of the toughest moments of their lives. While this doesn't always mean they will constantly be calm, it does mean that they will find and focus on their inner peace to try to find their calm, so they can think rationally and make the best decisions.

You aren't going to find peace by changing jobs or going back to school. You won't find peace by refusing to talk to certain people because they always bring drama into your life, though this can help. At the same time, if you feel that this isn't the right decision, then you need to find a way to deal with the stress and chaos they bring into your life. This might mean that you sit down and talk to them about what you are willing to listen to and what you are not. This isn't rude or disrespectful, this is simply protecting your emotional and psychological well-being.

The only true way you are going to reach your inner peace is by getting to know yourself better. To do this, you need to spend quality time with yourself - some people refer to this as "me time." This is when you are alone and doing something you love or thinking about your thoughts. You might spend your time thinking about everything that happened that day, what you can improve on, and what you did well. You might spend this time writing in your journal or reading a book about inspirational quotes. You can also spend this time focusing on your creative outlet to get to know yourself better. For example, you might write about how you feel and why. Some people will need more "me time" than other people. People who are highly sensitive or introverted will need more alone time than people who are outgoing and extroverted. It doesn't matter how much "me time" you need, what matters is that you maintain a healthy mindset. This means that you don't become too withdrawn and you don't become too overwhelmed. This is a line that is difficult to find, but once you do, you will feel happy, calm, and at peace. You will feel that you can handle more than you could before.

There are many ways that you can spend time alone. In fact, you already probably know some of your favorite ways to spend time alone. At the same time, you need to think of ways that will help you understand yourself better. This may mean you have a conversation with yourself. Ask yourself how your day went and how certain situations make you feel. If you have a problem, ask yourself what advice you would give a friend. Sit back and think about your day, simply reflect on everything that happened. Take a moment to think about the person you want to be and how your true inner peace feels and find ways to work toward reaching your best person as this will lead you to a fulfilling life.

Quote #4

"If there's no inner peace, people can't give it to you. The husband can't give it to you. Your children can't give it to you. You have to give it to you." - *Linda Evans (Sweatt, 2016)*.

No matter who we are or how many people we have around us that bring peace, we are not going to feel true peace until we fill our hearts with peace. Inner peace is not something that someone else can give you, it is something that you need to find on your own. Furthermore, you need to find your inner peace before you can truly spread peace to other people within your life. You aren't going to feel that your environment is peaceful until you feel inner peace.

It's important that we do not depend on other people to bring our inner peace. We should only depend on ourselves as no one else can truly understand the way we feel. No matter how hard we try to explain what we need to feel at peace, we are the only ones who completely understand what we need.

When you are working toward developing your inner peace, it is okay to be a little selfish. This might seem strange to say to some people, but there are always times in our lives, especially when it deals with our mental and emotional health, that we need to put other people aside, even our family, and focus on ourselves. This doesn't mean that you will go off on your own for days, it means that you take a few minutes and go for a drive. You take 10 minutes every morning, find a quiet place, and meditate. This isn't saying that the people around you can't help you feel more at peace, they always can. What the quote says is that you need to focus on you when it comes to your inner peace. You need to take time to learn how you can develop your inner peace. It might take a bit for you to find your best solution. You might also feel that you need to take time in the morning and in the evening. You need to do what you feel is right when focusing on your inner peace.

It is hard to explain this process to your family, especially younger children. Younger children are not going to understand whereas your significant other and older children will want to do what they can to help you. To help your family understand that you need time to develop your inner peace, express to them that they also need time to develop their inner peace. This isn't something that is specific to you. Everyone needs to focus on themselves when developing inner peace.

You will know when you start to reach your inner peace because you will feel more comfortable in your own skin. You will remain calm in times of crises and you will find that you have more patience to deal with the chaos of life. This isn't something that will happen overnight. You will also need to work on keeping your inner peace once you reach it. You can accomplish this by continuing your strategies, such as breathing exercises, meditation, reading a book, or listening to music.

Quote #5

"It isn't enough to talk about peace. One must believe in it. And it isn't enough to believe in it. One must work at it."

- Eleanor Roosevelt (Branch, 2015).

Peace isn't something that you will gain because you start talking about it. It won't happen just because you believe in it. Internal peace exists in your life when you take the time and work at it. Eleanor Roosevelt understood how hard it is to work at bringing peace into your life. Throughout her adult years, she focused on bringing peace into the world. She wanted nothing more than to see everyone feel the peace she felt in her heart and soul.

Some moments in your life are going to be harder, causing you to struggle creating a peaceful environment and peace within your heart. You will need to learn how to let go of your fears and accept what happens in your life. You need to change your mindset, focusing more on the positives within your environment than the negatives. Working toward peace means you are going to strive to keep peace inside of you every day of your life, even when someone or something is trying to break it down. Fortunately, once you reach your natural state of peace, a fire will burn inside of you and give you the energy to succeed in holding your peace together.

However, your job of working toward peace is not going to stop once you feel you have reached your internal peace. You will still need to work at keeping your peace - you always need to keep that peaceful fire burning. You need to work at reaching and keeping your peace every day of your life. While this might seem like a never-ending job, once you reach your peaceful state of mind, you will cradle it like a child and do anything to protect your peace. You won't feel like it is a job. Instead, it feels like a part of you, something you are proud of and want to hold on to.

The ways you can work to bring peace into your life are endless. For instance, you can start acting and speaking without fear or worries. Don't worry about what other people are going to think about what you say. You need to speak, so you can clear your mind and bring in more positivity. Forget about judging yourself and other people. Everyone is their own unique person and deserves to be treated with respect and compassion. If you wouldn't say something mean to someone else, don't say it to yourself. At the same time, you need to follow the "golden rule" and treat other people like you want to be treated.

There is always conflict in your life or within the world, but this doesn't mean you have to be a part of it. It's always up to you in what you do when conflict arises. You can choose to be the mediator and try to solve any problem rationally, or you can decide to play the blame game. You need to focus on what is best for you and your inner peace. You might find that the more you acknowledge conflict, state your opinions, listen to other people, and let it go, the more peaceful your life will become. Of course, this isn't going to be easy, and working for something - including your inner peace - isn't always easy. But it is always 100% worth it.

Quote #6

"The life of inner peace, being harmonious and without stress, is the easiest type of existence."

- *Norman Vincent Peale.*

No matter what life you lead, there are times of hardship and Peale understood this. His quote discusses how you need to overcome these hardships, handle them without stress and worry to reach your life of inner peace. Once you reach your peace, you will feel like you are soaring through life. You won't have your worries holding you down. You will feel like you can accomplish anything you set your mind to. As Peale stated, this is a very harmonious and easy life to live.

This is a dream for most people and one that they don't feel they can reach. This is one of the problems of reaching your inner peace - you don't believe you can have it. You don't believe it exists. After all, there is always something that is going to cause you stress or worry. You may feel there will always be money problems, no matter how hard you work. How can you reach your inner peace if you know there will always be something that will cause you stress? How can this be possible?

But it isn't always lack of money or problems at work that cause us stress. Sometimes, it's what is going on internally. For instance, you suffer from a psychological illness, like depression or anxiety. These factors are going to create a strong feeling of stress. You feel overwhelmed and get tired of the daily struggles you face trying to overcome mental illness.

The first step you need to take is knowing that

you can let go of all your stress and negative thoughts. It will take time and a lot of mindset changes, but it is completely possible. To do this, you need to think of these factors as emotional pain. It's not a thought that is wearing you down, it is a feeling that is causing you internal pain. It makes you feel overwhelmed, causing your emotions to take over your life.

There are four steps you can take to let go of your negative thoughts, stress, and emotional pain.

Change your negative thinking. Changing your mindset is essential when filling your life with peace. Every quote about peace looks at how you need to start your peaceful journey by changing your mindset and by letting go of your negative thinking and focusing on positive thoughts. Your negative thoughts might be about yourself, your career, how you keep your house, or other people. Negative thoughts take a lot of energy. In fact, they will suck you dry. Positive thoughts will give you energy and make you feel like you can take on the world. Stop yourself when you notice a negative thought and think of something positive. You don't need to think about the same topic, the point is to start by thinking about anything positive.

Don't take anything personally. People are good at personalizing everything toward themselves because our world revolves around us. No matter how much you don't want to admit it, your world does revolve around you. This is normal human thinking. It doesn't mean you don't think or care about other people. It means that what you are going through, what people tell you, and what people do to you matters in your life. If someone says something mean to you, don't let it internalize. Do your best to let it go and realize that they are just words. What another person thinks or says about you doesn't mean it is true. Focus on spreading compassion and love to other people and becoming your best self.

Forgive yourself and other people. You have probably heard the phrase that you should forgive people but not because they deserve your forgiveness. You want to forgive them for yourself. There is truth in this statement. By holding on to the pain someone caused, you're allowing them to control parts of your emotions and life. You are the only person who is in control of your life. You also need to forgive yourself for your mistakes. Learn from them and allow yourself to grow.

Love yourself unconditionally. There are many different types of love, but the type that people often crave is one that is hard to get, and this is unconditional love. It is never certain that someone else is going to love you unconditionally. Therefore, you need to focus on loving yourself in this manner. Take a moment every day to talk about how much you love yourself. This will lift your spirits and make you believe that anything is possible.

Through these four steps, you will let go of your emotional pain. It's at this moment, you will feel your stress decrease. Soon, you won't feel the stresses of life. Instead, you will feel at peace. You will believe you can handle anything that comes your way.

Quote #7

"We don't realize that, somewhere within us all, there does exist a supreme self who is eternally at peace."

- *Elizabeth Gilbert (A Place for Mom Staff, 2013).*

There are a few religions and ways of thinking, such as Buddhism and stoicism, that focus on finding your internal peace. In Buddhism, you focus on meditation, living simply, and following the ways of Buddha to find your internal peace. Stoicism focuses on envisioning your higher self, the best version of you, and reaching this person through your actions and thoughts.

While Buddhism and stoicism are different, they focus on one factor and that is reaching your best self; the version of you that is eternally at peace. This version of you can control emotions, allowing you to control your actions and thoughts. You know what you can't control and accept it. You change the pieces of your life you can control in order to reach your supreme self.

Your best self may be at peace because you give back to your community. You have your dream job and you don't allow yourself to worry about the future. Instead, you live in the present moment and understand that this is what matters.

You won't reach your supreme self overnight. It is going to take time, patience, and understanding. You need to work to change your mindset to reach your best self. One step to take is to bring peace in your mind and environment. With this peace, you will overcome your struggles, learn to live in the moment, and be happy with what you have in your life. You won't strive for more; you will strive to maintain your peace.

Controlling your emotions is one of the toughest steps to reaching your supreme self and peace. However, it is 100% in your control. Through mindful meditation, understanding you control your actions and thoughts, and accepting the pieces of your life that are beyond your control, you will gain power over your emotions. You will find yourself taking a deep breath when you become frustrated and instead of lashing out, you will feel relaxed and find a solution to the problem.

To help control your emotions, you can ask for guidance from a higher power, focus on healthy eating, exercise, understand and forgive your emotional triggers, and focus on positivity in your life.

Quote #8

"No person, no place, and no thing has any power over us, for 'we' are the only thinkers in our mind. When we create peace and harmony and balance in our minds, we will find it in our lives."

- *Louise L. Hay (Barrientos, 2019).*

Louis L. Hay explains you will not find peace until you create peace within your mind. In other words, you need to find your peace of mind. There is nothing that you can buy that will give you true peace. You might feel at peace when you bring in a new book, clothes, a crystal, or anything that makes you happy. But this is merely a mask that will come off in time. You can take your dream vacation and "get away" from the stress of life for a period of time, but nothing is going to truly change. When you come home, you will have your worries and stress waiting for you. Even your significant other or children can't bring you true peace within your mind. The only person that can is you.

There are many ways that you can start to find peace of mind. First, you need to trust yourself. Trust that things are always as they seem, and your struggles will get easier. You will overcome whatever is mentally and emotionally holding you down.

Second, you want to let go of some of your expectations. We all have high expectations of ourselves as we have this perfect vision of ourselves, we want to reach. Remember, perfection is impossible to reach. You are going to make mistakes. It's what you do with these mistakes that matters. For instance, instead of focusing on what you did wrong, you want to learn from your mistakes. Use them as a teaching tool, so you can continue to grow as a person.

Third, use the hope you have to focus on positivity. Positivity is like a magnet that you need to hold in your life every day. Become mindful of your thinking and when you have a negative thought, focus on a positive thought. One technique is to think of two positives thoughts for every negative thought. This will help retrain your mind to focus on positivity and bring you peace of mind.

Quote #9

"Peace is the result of retraining your mind to process life as it is, rather than as you think it should be."

- *Wayne W. Dyer.*

One of the biggest reasons people lack peace in their lives is because they worry. This is understandable as we have a lot going on in our lives. Some of us are trying to raise children in a world of social media, paying bills, working more than one job, struggling with our health, and thinking about our friends and family who are struggling. By looking at our busy lives, it is not surprising that psychological disorders, such as depression and anxiety are on the rise.

When we focus more on the worry and stress of our lives, we struggle to find our peace. We are focused on what is going to happen, rather than what is happening. We look at ways we can control every single piece of our life. This isn't because we have an overwhelming feeling of needing to be in control; it's because we are trying to find our true peace. We are trying to find our calm in the storm of life and the only way we can think to do this is through control.

It's time to stop focusing on control and focus more on what Wayne W. Dyer is saying in his uplifting quote. We need to understand what we can control and what we can't. There is very little we can control within our lives. We can control how our emotions and how we react to situations. We can control our decisions, what we say, and do. In general, we can only control ourselves and how we treat other people and our surroundings. Other people will control everything else that happens in our world.

In a sense, Dyer is telling us to "go with the flow" when it comes to events in our lives. We need to accept what is happening and focus on only what we can change. Once we follow this path in our lives, we will finally feel peace within ourselves. When this happens, we will believe our environment is peace, creating a stronger peace within our mind.

Quote #10

"Peace is a daily, a weekly, a monthly process, gradually changing opinions, slowly eroding old barriers, quietly building new structures."
- *John F. Kennedy.*

This quote comes from John F. Kennedy's last speech to the United Nations General Assembly on September 20, 1963. During a time when American society was torn with racism, Kennedy stepped into the oval office and worked to end segregation and racism in America. While some people despised his work, other people praised Kennedy and began focusing on creating more peace in the world.

One of the factors Kennedy knew about peace that he tried to teach the world was that peace won't happen overnight. Peace is something people have to work toward every day of their life. To bring peace into your life and the life of other people, you need to change your mindset. This is always a gradual process.

When Kennedy spoke of peace, he didn't just talk about peace inside of your home. He talked about creating more peace in society, meaning people had to change their opinions. They could no longer push for segregation or believe in the superiority of a race. American society had to learn from the past and not bring the past into the future. They had to tear down the walls that divided society to create this racism and segregation.

Once the old barriers disappeared, new walls would form. They would build themselves silently and gradually. Because people are striving to live in a more peaceful society every day, they wouldn't notice the positive changes happening right before their eyes. However, people would notice over time because their lives will feel more peaceful and they will focus on bringing peace into the lives of others.

To start creating a more peaceful world, we need to start at home. You need to start with your own mindset and then work toward bringing peace into the lives of other people. There are many ways to bring a stronger sense of peace in your life. For instance, you can start to meditate on a daily basis. Focusing on meditation will help you erase the negativity you feel on a daily basis. You will become more mindful, noticing what thoughts are floating around in your mind. Changing your negative thoughts into positive thoughts is one of the first steps to finding peace.

Another way to bring more peace into your life is by filling your world with peace. What you put out into the world will come back into your life. Therefore, if you focus on peace, your life will become more peaceful. If you focus on positivity, you will start to feel more positive. Focus on friends and family that bring positivity and peace in your life as they will help you focus on developing a peaceful mindset.

- -

Chapter 6: Conclusion

The purpose of this book is to help you overcome certain challenges in your life and reach your best self. This is the person that you strive to be. Your best self doesn't mean that you are perfect. It's important to remember that perfection doesn't exist. What your best self does is help you reach a fulfilling life.

Through these 50 quotes, you will find one to read every day and start to work toward fulfilling your life. You won't stop when you have read every quote in this book. Instead, you will find ways to continue to maintain your life of fulfillment. You should also realize that just because you feel you lead a fulfilling life doesn't mean that you can't expand this feeling. For example, you are single now, but in five years might be married with a child. Your family is going to expand your feeling of fulfillment by bringing in something new into your life.

Each of the emotions within the contents of this books is a large part of your life. Throughout your day, you are going to feel happiness. For most people, this is their main emotion. Therefore, it is one that you will work hard to include in your daily routine because it will lead you to a more fulfilling life more than any other emotion. But just because you feel happiness more throughout your life, doesn't mean you need to ignore your other emotions.

Every day you will find a challenge that you need to overcome. You may overcome these challenges in one day while other challenges will take you days, weeks, months, or even years. Because overcoming challenges is an important part of your life, it has made its way into this book. You need to understand that you can face our challenges and overcome them in order to reach your highest potential. Even if you feel that the challenge you see in front of you is your toughest yet, you will gain the belief and knowledge to overcome each one of your challenges.

Fear is one of the most powerful emotions that we feel. Whether we admit it, or even realize it, fear stops people from reaching their goals every day. Because we become so used to feeling afraid to take the next step, it becomes natural for us and we don't think about how much fear affects our lives and mindset. This book shows you that it is time to stop allowing your fears to control you and take charge of your fear. This means you need to learn to control your emotions, so your emotions don't control you.

One way you will work on controlling your emotions is through creating a peace of mind. When you feel inner peace, you are going to feel peace in your environment. Peace helps you understand situations better, allows you to remain calm, and helps you realize that better days are on the way.

Even if you are struggling, you will hold on to your peace and know that you can overcome this challenge. Continuing to hold your inner peace will help you spread peace into the world. Most people feel that the world could use a lot more peace. However, people can't really give peace until they feel peace inside of them. Therefore, to spread peace you need to reach your inner peace and stop depending on other people to help you feel at peace.

Death is unavoidable. No matter who you are, you will deal with the loss of someone you love at some point in your life. That is why this chapter is included and such an important piece of the puzzle. To lead a fulfilling life, you need to understand that grief is going to stay with you. Once someone you love passes away, a piece of you is always going to miss them. You might wish you could call them years after they have passed just so you can hear their voice. You may think of all the times they hugged you and how that made you feel. Because grief affects everyone differently, people are going to react in different ways. No matter how you react to grief, this book will help you through your process. You can take these quotes with you on your path as they will help you adjust, so you can continue to lead a fulfilling life.

Of course, there are many other emotions, both negative and positive, that you will feel throughout your life. Some of these emotions will keep you from feeling fulfilled while others will lead you into the world of fulfillment. No matter what emotion you are feeling, there are some key takeaways that you can focus on to help you overcome any negative emotions and thrive when you feel positively.

First, you always need to accept your emotions. This is easier when you feel a positive emotion over negative. But, no matter how you are feeling, you need to accept it in order to move to the next step.

Second, you need to face your emotions. This is going to be a challenge when you are dealing with a negative emotion, but it is essential. If you don't face your emotion, you won't understand why you are feeling this way. Instead, you will try to push the emotion aside or ignore it. No matter what you have been told in your life, ignoring your emotions is never going to help you. In fact, it will only cause you more problems.

Third, you need to look deeper into your emotion. You can do this by asking yourself a series of questions, such as why you feel this way or what you can do to change the way you are feeling. When it comes to this step, you need to be honest with yourself. Honesty is the only true way you are going to help yourself.

Fourth, you need to let go, especially the negative emotions. To do this, you might need to practice forgiveness for yourself and other people. This is going to be hard and you will find yourself going back and forth on your emotions from time to time. But, as long as you follow the previous steps, you will be able to let go of your emotions and move on toward your best self.

Finally, be proud of yourself. It takes a lot of work to reach a fulfilling life. It also takes a lot of time and patience when it comes to making sure you continue to maintain this lifestyle. It's not something everyone reaches in their lifetime, so when you finally feel you can reach your fulfilling life, be proud of yourself.

- -

References

- - - - - - - - -

1. 5 steps to overcome fear. (n.d.). Retrieved 30 September 2019, from https://www.thetoolsbook.com/blog/2017/7/9/5-steps-to-overcome-fear.

2. 20 quotes about grief. (2018). Retrieved 1 October 2019, from https://everloved.com/articles/living-with-grief/20-grief-quotes/.

3. 20 self-love quotes to inspire more positivity and strong self-esteem. (n.d.). Retrieved 1 October 2019, from https://www.notsalmon.com/2015/11/18/positive-quotes-about-self-love/

4. 67 quotes about overcoming adversity and challenges in your life. (2019). Retrieved 1

October 2019, from https://
www.happierhuman.com/quotes-about-
overcoming-adversity/

5. A David C. Hill quote. (n.d.). Retrieved 1
October 2019, from https://
www.treasurequotes.com/quotes/we-cant-
control-the-world-we-can-only-barely-control-
our-own-reactions-to-it-happiness-is-larg

6. A Place for Mom Staff. (2013). "There does
exist a supreme self who is eternally at peace."
Retrieved 30 September 2019, from https://
www.aplaceformom.com/blog/eternally-at-
piece/

7. A quote by Abraham Lincoln. (n.d.).
Retrieved 1 October 2019, from https://
www.goodreads.com/quotes/69-folks-are-

usually-about-as-happy-as-they-make-their/

8. A quote by Gautama Buddha. (n.d.). Retrieved 1 October 2019, from https://www.goodreads.com/quotes/1289176-thousands-of-candles-can-be-lit-from-a-single-candle

9. A quote by Helen Keller. (n.d.). Retrieved 1 October 2019, from https://www.goodreads.com/quotes/3443-when-one-door-of-happiness-closes-another-opens-but-often

10. A quote by John F. Kennedy. (n.d.). Retrieved 30 September 2019, from https://www.goodreads.com/quotes/102477-peace-is-a-daily-a-weekly-a-monthly-process-gradually

11. A quote by Marthe Troly-Curtin. (n.d.). Retrieved 1 October 2019, from https://www.goodreads.com/quotes/29449-time-you-enjoy-wasting-is-not-wasted-time

12. A quote by Roger Crawford. (n.d.). Retrieved 1 October 2019, from https://www.goodreads.com/quotes/496796-being-challenged-in-life-is-inevitable-being-defeated-is-optional

13. Acosta, G. (2014). 30 inspirational quotes for when the going gets tough - blog | USC's online MSW. Retrieved 1 October 2019, from https://msw.usc.edu/mswusc-blog/31-inspirational-quotes-for-when-the-going-gets-tough/

14. Barrientos, S. (2019). 20 quotes about

peace that will calm your mind. Retrieved 30
September 2019, from https://
www.goodhousekeeping.com/life/a27115824/
peace-quotes/

15. Bernie Siegel Quotes. (n.d.). Retrieved 1
October 2019, from https://
www.brainyquote.com/quotes/
bernie_siegel_607643

16. Branch, M. (2015). 10 inspiring Eleanor
Roosevelt quotes | unfoundation.org. Retrieved
30 September 2019, from https://
unfoundation.org/blog/post/10-inspiring-
eleanor-roosevelt-quotes/

17. Chernoff, A. (n.d.). 9 ways to find peace of
mind in tough times. Retrieved 30 September
2019, from https://www.marcandangel.com/

2013/05/09/9-ways-to-find-peace-in-tough-times/

18. Dryer. (n.d.) Retrieved 30 September 2019, from https://www.passiton.com/inspirational-quotes/7431-peace-is-the-result-of-retraining-your-mind-to

19. Edberg, H. (2019). 73 inspirational quotes on fear [updated for 2019]. Retrieved 1 October 2019, from https://www.positivityblog.com/22-inspirational-quotes-on-fear/

20. Fulmore, A. (n. d.). 4 steps to let go of stress, negativity, and emotional pain. Retrieved 30 September 2019, from https://tinybuddha.com/blog/steps-let-go-stress-negativity-emotional-pain/

21. Godin, S. (n. d.). Being aware of your fear is smart. Overcoming it is the mark of a successful person. - Positively Positive. Retrieved 1 October 2019, from https://www.positivelypositive.com/quotes/being-aware-of-your-fear-is-smart-overcoming-it-is-the-mark-of-a-successful-person/

22. Jim Rohn quotes. (n.d.). Retrieved 1 October 2019, from https://www.brainyquote.com/quotes/jim_rohn_147498

23. Joseph B. Wirthlin quotes. (n.d.). Retrieved 1 October 2019, from https://www.brainyquote.com/quotes/joseph_b_wirthlin_646016

24. Joshua J. Marine quotes. (n.d.). Retrieved 1 October 2019, from http://www.quoteland.com/

author/Joshua-J-Marine-Quotes/805/

25. Life quotes. (n.d.). Retrieved 1 October 2019, from https://www.pinterest.com/ wordstobreathe/life-quotes/

26. Lupita Nyong'o quotes. (n.d.). Retrieved 1 October 2019, from https:// www.brainyquote.com/quotes/ lupita_nyongo_601366

27. Maraboli, S. (n.d.). Cry. Forgive. Learn. Move on. Let your tears water the seeds of your future happiness. - tiny buddha. Retrieved 1 October 2019, from https://tinybuddha.com/ wisdom-quotes/cry-forgive-learn-move-let-tears-water-seeds-future-happiness/

28. Marianne Williamson quotes. (n.d.).

Retrieved 1 October 2019, from https://www.brainyquote.com/quotes/marianne_williamson_385965

29. Mort, J. (2015). 21 absolutely heart wrenching quotes on loss and grief. Retrieved 1 October 2019, from https://thoughtcatalog.com/johanna-mort/2015/05/21-absolutely-heartwrenching-quotes-on-loss-and-grief/

30. Motivation Mondays: Power of gratitude. (2019). Retrieved 1 October 2019, from https://mirthandmotivation.com/2019/01/14/motivation-mondays-power-of-gratitude/

31. Motivational cards riversongs Messages of hope greeting cards. (n.d.). Retrieved 1 October 2019, from https://www.riversongs.com/

motivational-ecards-hope-cards.html

32. Norman Vincent Peale quotes. (n.d.). Retrieved 30 September 2019, from https://www.brainyquote.com/quotes/norman_vincent_peale_121775

33. Raymond, C. (2019). 20 insightful, moving quotes about grief and loss. Retrieved 1 October 2019, from https://www.verywellhealth.com/grief-loss-and-mourning-quotes-1132589

34. Richard Jefferies quotes. (n.d.). Retrieved 1 October 2019, from https://www.brainyquote.com/quotes/richard_jefferies_629192

35. Scott, A. (2017). W. Clement Stone - Travel quote of the week - Authentic traveling.

Retrieved 1 October 2019, from https://authentictraveling.com/travel-thoughts/travel-quote-of-the-week-january-10-2017/

36. Sedulia. (2013). Kübler-Ross: The reality is that you will grieve forever. Retrieved 1 October 2019, from https://www.consolatio.com/2013/09/k%C3%BCbler-ross-the-reality-is-that-you-will-grieve-forever.html

37. Sweatt, L. (2016). 17 quotes about finding inner peace. Retrieved 30 September 2019, from https://www.success.com/17-quotes-about-finding-inner-peace/

38. Sweatt, L. (2016). 19 quotes about facing your fears. Retrieved 30 September 2019, from https://www.success.com/19-quotes-about-facing-your-fears/

39. Terri Irwin quotes. (n.d.). Retrieved 1 October 2019, from https://www.brainyquote.com/quotes/terri_irwin_902544

40. Zwarensteyn, J. (2018). 25 encouraging quotes to share with someone who is grieving the loss of a loved one. Retrieved 1 October 2019, from https://www.yourtango.com/2018319423/best-grief-quotes-support-someome-experiencing-stages-of-grief.

- -

Printed in Great Britain
by Amazon